EMOTIONAL INTELLIGENCE OF ADOLESCENTS

EMOTIONAL INTELLIGENCE OF ADOLESCENTS

By

Dr. R.K. Adsul

Associate Professor & Head
Department of Psychology
Smt. Mathubai Garware Kanya Mahavidyalaya
Sangli Maharashtra
(INDIA)

DISCOVERY PUBLISHING HOUSE PVT. LTD.
NEW DELHI-110 002

Published by:
Tilak Wasan

DISCOVERY PUBLISHING HOUSE PVT. LTD.
4383/4B, Ansari Road, Darya Ganj
New Delhi-110 002 (India)
Phone : +91-11-23279245, 43596064-65
Fax : +91-11-23253475
E-mail : discoverypublishinghouse@gmail.com
sales@discoverypublishinggroup.com

web : www.discoverypublishinggroup.com

***First Edition:* 2015**

ISBN: 978-93-5056-725-8

Emotional Intelligence of Adolescents

Printed at:
Infinity Imaging Systems
Delhi

Dedicated
to

Dr. R.R. BORUDE *(Psychologist)*
Aurangabad

Dr. C.G. DESHPANDE
(Psychologist & My Teacher)
Pune

Dr. D.S. JANBANDHU *(My Guide)*
Nagpur

for their Kind Blessings

PREFACE

Emotional intelligence plays a key role in determine life success of adolescents. It is the ability to identify, use, understand and manage emotions in positive ways to relieve stress, communicate effectively, and empathize with others, overcome challenges and diffuse conflicts. Emotional Intelligence impacts many different aspects of adolescents daily life, such as the way they behave and the way they interact with others. Emotional intelligence involves the ability to perceive accurately, appraise and express emotions, the ability to access and or generate feelings when they facilitate through, the ability to understand emotions and emotional knowledge, and the regulate emotions to promote emotional and intellectual growth (Mayer and Salovy, 1997).

In brief we can say that emotional intelligence refers to emotional reasoning used to understand and manage the expressions of emotions of self and others. Thus emotional intelligence is an umbrella term that captures a broad collection of interpersonal and intrapersonal skills.

School is a place where students get together share instructions and social infrastructures, which is fundamental in shaping their interests, attitudes and habits. Many activities in the classroom have an influence on the student's personality. School climate is an important input for building the healthy learning environment. The school is the major socialization institution for any child. It is the child's first contract with the world outside the house. For nearly 12 years a child spends

5 to 7 hours a day in the school. School is one of the most important foundation pillars on which the child's personality develops. Children learn proficiencies in various abilities like: learning process and home work, social communications, handling emotions and the management of day-to-day interactions at home and schools. Academic climate also affects on emotional intelligence of adolescents.

Parental attitude plays an important role in development of emotional intelligence of adolescents. Parental acceptance attitude shows the love for the child. The accepting parent put the child in a position of importance in the home and develops a relationship of emotional warmth. They encourage the child and make itself apparent in receptive or positive attitude towards the child's idea and judgments, worthiness and capability, love and affection and admiration along with adequate attention towards him. An avoidance attitude of parents manifests itself in interpersonal relationships in direct ways, when the child has to face excessive criticism, jealousy comparison, harsh and inconsistent punishment by both or either of the parents in his upbringing. An avoidance attitude of parents may also exhibit itself in physical neglect, denial of love and affection, lack of interest in his activities and failure to spend time with him. Concentration or protection in the child makes him better and more confident. Reality is that over-protection is a disease and obstructs the independent growth of the child. But sense of protection gives the child strength and psychological support. So the sense of protection and over protection both are different. In over protection which consists in excessive contact of parents with the child, such as fondling him or sleeping with him, prolongation of infantile care as nursing, bathing and dressing when child can do it itself, prevention of the growth of self-reliance by supervising the child's activities too much and defending him or solving his problems. Parent shows over anxiousness towards the child's health and protection him from strong participation in completing activities. Thus overprotection signifies giving more care to their child than what is necessary and can only be deemed as the hyper state of protection.

We may be inclined to regard well-adjusted adolescents who are psychologically comfortable and who experience very little distress. Everyone at some time likely has experienced fear, anxiety and depression of mood unsolved or unsolvable problems. But good adjusted person copes well with his personal problems.

Present study is conducted to examine the effects of family relationship and academic climate on emotional intelligence and adjustment of adolescents. It is found that a parental acceptance level significantly affects emotional intelligence of adolescents. Parental high acceptance attitude increases emotional intelligence than average and low level of parental acceptance attitude. Parental concentration attitude are significantly different on emotional intelligence. Level of PC affects EI. High PC creates low EI and low PC supports to development of EI in adolescents. Parental avoidance attitude (PV) significantly affects emotional intelligence of adolescents. It is found that high PV negatively influence on development of EI of adolescents. It is also found that levels of Academic Climate (AC) significantly affect EI. It means that high AC creates high EI, while low AC creates low EI of adolescents. Levels of AC significantly affect adjustment of adolescents. It means that high AC supports good adjustment, while low AC results poor adjustment of adolescents. It is also found that there is significant effect of family relationships on adjustment of adolescents.

This study would be a great use of educational planners, administrators, institutional heads, Psychological councellors and teachers along with parents and society.

It is my duty to express sense of gratitude towards all those who helped me in various stages of this work. I am also grateful to the sample students for this kind co-operation and valuable responses.

I am indebted to Discovery Publishing House Pvt. Ltd., New Delhi for publishing this book with all care.

— Author

ACKNOWLEDGEMENTS

After completion of my book *' Emotional Intelligence of Adolescents'* it is my duty to express sense of gratitude towards all those who helped me at the various stages of this work.

I have a great pleasure to express my deep sense of gratitude to University Grants Commission, New Delhi for sponsoring the Major Research project "Effect of family relationship and academic climate on emotional intelligence and adjustment of adolescents" and granting the financial assistance.

I have a great pleasure to express my deep sense of gratitude to Dr. R.G. Kulkarni, Principal, Smt. Mathubai Garware Kanya Mahavidyalaya, Sangli, Dr. D.S. Janbandhu (Nagpur), Dr. R.R. Borude (Aurangabad), Dr. C.G. Deshpande (Pune), Prin. P.J. Tahamankar, Prof. S.B. Mangavakar, Prof. A.C. Date for their guidance and constant encouragement, while completing this Major Research Project.

I would like to pay due respect and regards to Mr. Subodh Joshi, Associate Professor in English, for his reading of the manuscript and suggestions.

I would like to appreciate co-operation of Dr. V.S. Kamble, Asstt. Prof. in Psychology, K.W.C. Sangli, Project fellow Mr. Rahul Kamble, Mr. J.R. Patil, Mr. Vatan Bhosale, Mr. Shashikant Pisal, Mr. M.S. Suryawanshi, Mr. S. Kharat, Mr. S.S. Jadhav, all my colleagues in the Smt. M.G. Kanya

Mahavidyalaya and the Principals and headmasters/headmistress, teachers who gladly provided the data for the Major Research Project.

I express my deep sense of gratitude towards Dr. A.S. Parit, Dr. Bharat Naik, Principal Dr. L.K. Shitole (Pune), Dr. V.R. Shinde (Nasik), Dr. K.M. Jadhav (Baramati) and Dr. Tajane (Aurangabad) who supplied me valuable information through their interviews.

I am also grateful to sample students for their kind co-operation and valuable responses. Librarians and staff of Shivaji University Library, Kolhapur and Pune University, Pune provided the best possible facilities, I am thankful to them.

Co-operation and understanding of my family members were of great importance. Without that it was impossible for me to complete this work. I shall prefer to be indebted to them.

Dr. R.K. Adsul

CONTENTS

CONTENTS

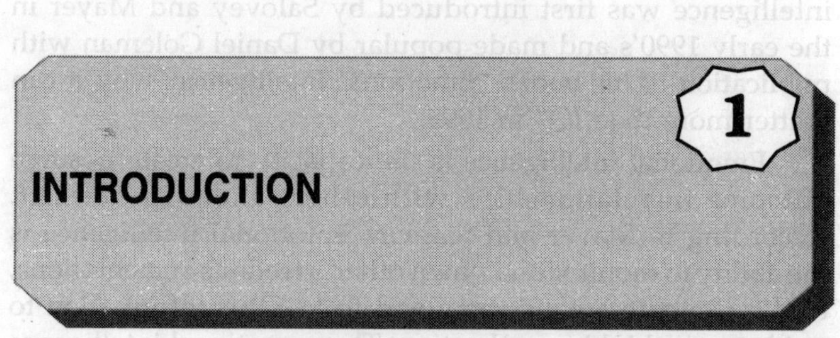

1 INTRODUCTION

Overview

Family is regarded as a nursery of socialization. The foundation of personality lies in the womb of family. In the present scenario, due to rapid socio-cultural changes in the society parent – child relation becoming complex, which affects on adolescents emotional intelligence and adjustment.

Emotional development in adolescents stems from their interaction at home with parents and siblings. Parent – child interaction and parent's way to deal with their children or develop certain attitude among children which group their relationships and interactions at home and outside.

There are hundreds of researches who have tried to study parent – child relationship. There are parents who treat their children, either with harsh discipline or empathic under standing, with indifference or warmth, with love or rejection. All these attitude adapted towards child rearing practices have deep and lasting consequences on child's emotional life.

Adolescents may be faced with serious problems to adjustment when there is difference of opinions, ideals and attitudes with their parents. Conflict may arise between the adolescents and the parents that are difficult to resolve.

Over the past 15 years the term emotional intelligence has received much attention as a factor that is useful in understanding and predicting individual's performance at work, at home at school etc. The concept of emotional intelligence was first introduced by Salovey and Mayer in the early 1990's and made popular by Daniel Goleman with publication of his books "Emotional Intelligence: why it can matter more than IQ" in 1995.

Emotional intelligence is the capacity to create positive outcome in relationships with others and with oneself. According to Mayer and Salovey, emotional intelligence is the ability to monitor one's own other's feelings and emotions, to discriminate among them and to use this information to guide one's thinking and action. Thus emotional intelligence is an umbrella term that captures a broad collection of interpersonal and intra-personal skills. Emotional intelligence plays a key role in determine life success healthy family relations develop emotional intelligence of adolescents.

Academic climate or school climate is a significant element in academic performance and personality development of adolescents. It is also related to inter-student conflicts, suicide, character education and moral education.

Haynes, Emmons and Ben-Avie (1997) suggested 15 key components of healthy, supportive school climate: achievement motivation, collaborative decision-making, equity and fairness, general school climate, order and discipline, parent involvement, school – community relations, staff dedication to students learning, staff expectations, leadership, school building, sharing of resources, caring and sensitivity, student interpersonal relations, students – teacher relations. The quality and consistency of inter personal interactions with the school community that influence adolescent's cognitive social and psychological development. At school, children cultivate interpersonal skills, discover and refine values and struggle with vulnerabilities. Academic climate help, the students to develop emotional intelligence and adjustment.

Statement of the Problem

From last six months in Maharashtra, there are number of school and college adolescents ended their life by committing suicide. It is a burning problem in Maharashtra. News papers and experts stated the causes of suicide that is, conflicts in school, academic stress, school and family mal-adjustment etc. These causes are related to family relationship and academic climate of adolescents. These affects an emotional intelligence and adjustment of adolescents. This problem is selected due to curiosity to see the effect of family relationship and academic climate on the emotional intelligence and adjustment.

In the past, many research studies were conducted on family relationship and emotional intelligence, family relationships and adjustment, emotional intelligence and adjustment, school climate and student's adjustment. But researcher found that not a single study has covered on effect of family relationship and academic climate on emotional intelligence and adjustment of adolescents. Hence, the researcher has selected this problem for study.

The Concept of Family Relationship

Family is an important institution in development of human personality. It is a support group for child forits mental development. Family gives love, affection, security and sense of belonging to children. Family provides financial assistance to their children. Parents are the first teacher and role models of their children.

Family being the first and major agency of socialization plays a pivotal role in shaping child's life. It has been shown that most of the children who are successful and well-adjusted come from families where healthy relationships exit between children and their parents. Family is the first environment place where child feels, observes and learns the emotional relationships (Warhol, 1998). Children try to understand the emotions through the attachment and modeling with parents (Denham *et al*. 2000).

The family provides the first context for recognition and communication of affective messages to develop social intelligence and social competence.

According to Morris *et al.* (2007) family environment affects children's emotional intelligence in three aspects. *Firstly,* child learns emotions by observing the people around them. *Secondly,* their experiences and behaviours related to parent's emotions ensure children to become appropriate to society's expectations. *Thirdly,* factors reflecting the emotional status of family such as the quality of emotional attachment between the child and the attitude of parents, emotional, social and marital relationship have impacts on emotional intelligence.

Definition

John Scanzoni and Colleagues (1989) in their attempt to expand definition of the family in the 1980's, discussed the traditional family defined as two parents and a child or children as the prevailing paradigm of the family.

The family is generally regarded as a major social institution and a locus of match of a person's social activity. It is a social unit created by blood, marriage or adoption and can be described as nuclear (Parents and Children) or extended (encompassing other relatives).

It is generally assumed today that the modern family has undergone significant transformations in its structure. We are told that societal changes have contributed to a sharp reduction in the percentage of classical 'typical' families principally 'nuclear' families.

The family is the oldest and the most important of all the institutions that man has devised to regulate and integrate his behaviour as he strives to satisfy his basic needs.

Fields and Casper (2001) The family is defined in censuses and surveys as two or more persons related by blood, marriage or adoption and living in the same residence. The first part of the definition excludes non-marital cohabitation but can include extended as well as nuclear family members. However, the second part of the definition severely restricts family composition by limiting the family members to those who share living facilities under the same roof (Glick, 1957).

The Importance of Family Relationship

Positive relationship between parents and their children can help to protect youth from engaging risky behaviour. Parents who are emotionally supportive and warm with their children they are less likely to use substance as such as alcohol or marijuana or engage in delinquent behaviour.

Friends can come and go however, family is here for life. It is so important that a family maintains close relations. Most important the relationship that exists between parents and children. Parents need to spend as much time as possible with their children.

Parents must let their children know that they love them and will always be there to talk to. Parent's communication is particularly important during the teenage years.

The teen years can be a hard time for children; many issues suddenly arise such as sex, dating and overall identity issues. Parents should communicate to their teens. The saying 'a family that prays together stays together.'

Family Relationships in India

Indians are giving strong values for family relationships. It is our culture that has been followed from olden days an earlier days and in some parts of India still, there are joint families.

Joint Families comprise many people – father, mother, children, grand parents, grand children etc. In these families there will be strict hierarchy.

The elder person in the family will be the master of the family. Ladies do household works, look after their children, and take care of their husband and parents etc. There will be a number of children in a joint family. They will learn to share what they have with others, to love and respect elders, to adjust themselves to the society or others from their younger age.

Nuclear Family

But now-a-day the number of joint families is getting decreasing. Parents are working. Children are studying apart from their parents. They can't always stay together with their grandparents. Thus the concept of nuclear families has emerged.

In nuclear families, there will be father, mother and at most two children. The Parents take care of their children. Also the income of parents is more compared to those in olden days. So children are giving better education. Children are compared and they are given what they want. As there is only a single or at most two children they needn't have to share anything with others.

Types of Parent – Child Relationships

(i) *Secure Relationships:* This is the strongest type of attachment. A child in this category feels he can depend on his parents. He knows that parents will be there when he needs support. The secure child usually plays well with other children his age.

(ii) *Avoidant Relationships:* Avoidant children have learned that depending on parents won't get them that, secure feeding they want, so they learn to take care of themselves. Avoidant children may seem too independent. Avoidant children do not build strong relationships with their parents.

(iii) *Ambivalent Relationships:* Ambivalence is another way of child may be insecurely attached to his parents. Children who are ambivalent have learned that sometimes their need met , and sometimes they are not. They notice what behaviour got their parents attention in the past and use it over and over.

(iv) *Disorganized Relationships*: Disorganized children don't know what to expect from their parents. Disorganized children will do things that seem to make no sense. The parents rarely respond to their needs. Children may have one or more parents suffering from depression.

Acceptance Attitude of Parents

The Warmth, affection, care, comfort, concern, nurturance, support or simply love that parents can feel and express towards their children. It has two principal expressions: *(i)* physical and *(ii)* verbal.

Physical expressions of parental acceptance include hugging, fondling, caressing, approving glances, kissing, smiling and other such indications of affection, approval or support.

Expressions of verbal include praising, complimenting, saying nice things to or about the child, perhaps singing songs or telling stories to a young child and the like.

Parental acceptance implies an attitude of love for the child. The accepting parent put the child in a position of importance in the home and develops a relationship of emotional warmth. Parental acceptance encourages the child and makes itself apparent in receptive or positive attitude towards the child's idea and judgments, worthiness and capability, love and affection and admiration along with adequate attention towards him.

Avoidance Attitude of Parents

This attitude of parents implies conditional love, recognizing that child has no right as a person, no right to express his feelings, no right to uniqueness and no right to become autonomous individual. An avoidance component of the home environment was found to be unrelated with high and low level of achievement motivation.

A child develops an unpleasant attitude when he does not find proper care and response of his parents. It is quite natural that a child meets proper nourishment of his genuine feeling. Denial of love and affection freezes the natural behaviour of child.

An avoidance attitude of parents manifests itself in interpersonal relationships in direct ways, when the child has to face excessive criticism, jealousy comparison, harsh and inconsistent punishment by both or either of the parents in his upbringing. An avoidance attitude of parents may also exhibit itself in physical neglect, denial of love and affection, lack of interest in his activities and failure to spend time with him.

Concentration (Overprotection) Attitude of Parents

Protection in the child makes him better and more confident. Reality is that over-protection is a disease and obstructs the independent growth of the child. But sense of protection gives the child strength and psychological support. So the sense of protection and over protection both are different. In overprotection which consists in excessive contact of parents with the child, such as fondling him or sleeping with him, prolongation of infantile care as nursing, bathing and dressing when child can do it itself, prevention of the growth of self-reliance by supervising the child's activities too much and defending him or solving his problems. Parent shows over anxiousness towards the child's health and protection him from strong participation in completing activities. Thus overprotection signifies giving more care to their child than what is necessary and can only be deemed as the hyper state of protection.

The Concept of Academic Climate

From almost one hundred years, educations have appreciated the importance of school climate. In 1908, Perry was the first educational leader to explicitly write about how school climate affects on students and the process of learning. Although Dewey did not write explicitly about school climate, his focus was on the social dimensions of school life and the notion that school should focus on enhancing the skills, knowledge and dispositions that support engaged democratic citizens (Dewey, 1927) implicitly touch on what kind of environment or climate the school reflects.

The school is the major socialization institution for any child. It is the child's first contract with the world outside the house. For nearly 12 years a child spends 5 to 7 hours a day in the school. School is one of the most important foundation pillars on which the child's personality develops. Children learn proficiencies in various abilities like learning process and home work, social communications, handling emotions and the management of day-to-day interactions at home and schools.

School is a place where students get together share instructions and social infrastructures, which is fundamental in shaping their interests, attitudes and habits. Many activities in the classroom have an influence on the student's personality. School climate is an important input for building the healthy learning environment. A stimulating educational environment responsive to the needs of the individual can result in positive motivational consequences. On the contrary negative motivational consequences will result if the environment is not facilitative (Chen, 2005; Brock, Nishidk, Choing, Grimm, Rimm – Kaufman, 2008).

Psychological Environment of School

The work of Maehr (1990) is very important. He worked on psychological environment of the school. He gave some dimensions of psychological environment of the school.

1. *Accomplishment:* Emphasis on excellence and pursuit of academic challenges.
2. *Power:* Emphasis on interpersonal competition, social comparison and achievement.
3. *Recognition:* Emphasis on social recognition for achievement and the importance of school for attaining future goals and rewards.
4. *Affiliation:* Perceived sense of community, good inter personal relationship among teachers and students.
5. *Strength/Saliency:* The perception that the school knows what it is about and that students know what is expected.

School Climate

Schools climate refers to the quality and charter of school life. School climate is based on patterns of students, parents and school personnel's experience of school life and reflects norms, goals, values, interpersonal relationships, teaching and learning practices and organizational structures.

Importance of School Climate

School climate can attract various areas and people within schools. Kuperminc *et al.* (1997) reported that positive school climate has been associated with fewer behavioural and emotional problems for students.

Hayens and Comer (1993) found that a positive, supportive and culturally conscious school climate can significantly shape the degree of academic success experienced by urban students.

McEvoy and Welker (2000) mentioned that positive interpersonal relationships and optimal learning opportunities for students in all demographic environments can increase achievement levels and reduce maladaptive behaviour.

Schools climate can play a significant role in providing a healthy and positive school atmosphere.

Freiberg (1998) Suggested that a positive school climate can yield positive educational and psychological outcomes for students and school personnel.

Manning and Saddlemire (1996) conclude aspects of school climate, including trust, respect, mutual obligation and concern for others welfare can have powerful effects on educator's and learners' interpersonal relationships as well as learns academic achievement and over all school progress.

Importance of Teacher – Student Relationships

Teacher – student relationships are important to virtually all students. However, high quality teacher – student relationships appear to be most significant for children who are 'at risk' for school failure (Baker, 2006). In one study, high quality teacher – student relationship appeared to be better predicators of classroom adjustment, social skills and reading performances for children showing initial externalizing problems (*e.g.*, aggression, hyperactivity) internalizing problems (*e.g.*, attention) than for children without these initial risk factors (Baker, 2006).

Teacher – Student Relationship

Teacher can do –

1. To make an effort to get know each student in your classroom. Always call them by their names and strive to understand what they need to success in school (Croninger and Lee, 2001).
2. Make an efforts to spend time individually with each student, especially those who are difficult or shy. This

will help you create a more positive relationship with them (Rudasill, Rimm-Kaufman, Justice and Pence 2006).

3. Be aware of the explicit and implicit messages you are giving to your students (Rimm-Kaufman *et al*. 2002).
4. Create a positive climate in your classroom by focusing not only improving your relationships with your students, but also on enhancing the relationships among your students (Donahue *el al*. 2003).

The Concept of Emotional Intelligence

In 1966 German Psychiatrist named Leuner wrote an article called 'Emotional intelligence and emancipation.' He was hypothesized that some women willfully rejected the social roles and responsibilities because of their low emotional intelligence.

In 1983, Howard Gardner published a book named 'Frames of mind.' In this book he maintained that the dominant forms of intelligence associated with linguistic, logical and mathematical ability should be supplemented by five others. The new intelligence included (as well as musical, spatial and kinesthetic intelligences), interpersonal and intrapersonal intelligence.

Interpersonal intelligence means, the ability to understand people, what motivates them, how they work, how to work and co-operatively with them. Intrapersonal intelligence means "access to one's own feeling life, and the capacity to from an accurate, vertical model of oneself, and to be able to use that model to operate effectively in life.

In 1990, John Mayer and Peter Salovey and their colleagues published two articles that introduced the term 'Emotional intelligence'.

In 1995, Psychology Journalist Daniel Goleman wrote a book, 'Emotional intelligence'. Goleman brought together the existing body of emotional intelligence research with an introduction to how emotion works in the brain and added some practical examples of how emotional intelligence was being cultivated in schools and work places around USA.

In 1998, he published 'Working with Emotional Intelligence'. He included many things for expansion of emotional intelligence like 'self-confidence', 'trustworthiness', 'initiative', 'optimism', 'political awareness', 'leadership' and 'influence' and negotiation skills'.

According to Goleman, emotional intelligence refers to the ability to recognize and regulate emotions in ourselves and others. Salovy and Mayer (1997) defined, emotional intelligence "the ability to perceive emotion, integrate emotions and to facilitate thought, understand emotions and to regulate emotions to promote personal growth.

Bar-on (1997) explained emotional intelligence an array of non-cognitive abilities competencies and skills that influence one's ability to succeed in coping with environmental demands and pressures.

In brief we can say that emotional intelligence refers to emotional reasoning used to understand and manage the expressions of emotions of self and others.

Emotional intelligence involves the ability to perceive accurately, appraise and express emotions, the ability to access and or generate feelings when they facilitate through, the ability to understand emotions and emotional knowledge, and the regulate emotions to promote emotional and intellectual growth (Mayer and Salovy, 1997).

What is Emotional Intelligence?

Emotional Intelligence is the ability to identify, use, understand and manage emotions in positive ways to relieve stress, communicate effectively, and empathize with others, overcome challenges and diffuse conflicts. Emotional Intelligence impacts many different aspects of your daily life, such as the way you behave and the way you interact with others.

If you have high emotional Intelligence you are able to recognize your own emotional state and the emotional states of others. And engage with people in a way that draws them to you.

Emotional Intelligence Consisting of four Attributes

(i) *Self-awareness:* You recognize your own emotions and how they affect your thoughts and behaviour, know your strengths and weaknesses, and have self-confidence.

(ii) *Self-management:* You are able to control impulsive feelings and behaviours, manage your emotions in healthy ways, take initiative, follow through on commitments and adapt to changing circumstances.

(iii) *Social-awareness:* You can understand the emotions, needs and concerns of other people, pick up on emotional cues, feel comfortable socially and recognize the power dynamics in a group or organization.

(iv) *Relationship Management:* You know how to develop and maintain good relationships, communicate clearly, inspire and influence others, work well in a team and manage conflict.

Intelligence Quotient (IQ) vs. Emotional Quotient (EQ)

Intelligence Quotient (IQ) is a value that indicates a person's ability to learn, understand and apply information and skills in a meaningful way. Whereas Emotional Quotient (EQ) is way to measure how a person recognizes emotions in himself or herself and others, and manage these emotional states to work better as a group or team. A person has high EQ mean he is self-confident, self aware and able to handle difficult emotional experiences. He can recognize and control their own emotions and recognize others emotions to adjust their behaviour accordingly.

IQ can be measured by logical reasoning, word comprehension and mathematical skills rather than creative potential or emotional abilities. People with high IQ may be able to learn certain subjects very quickly and make connection between ideas and perceived things. They are academically successful.

Emotional Intelligence is more difficult to measure than IQ. The first modern IQ test was developed in 1905, but EQ test really was not developed until the 1990. Teachers and counselors at schools can administer IQ tests to see if student are having difficulties in class due to being two advanced or behind when compared to their peers. EQ tests are often used in education to help those students who may need special assistance in learning to manage their emotions or to better communicate with others.

Psychologists Contribute to Emotional Intelligence

Thorndike (1920)

According to the greatest S-R theorist Thorndike, social intelligence in one of the components of intelligence. He defined, social intelligence as the ability to understand and manage men and women, boys and girls to act wisely in human relations.

Gardner (1983)

Proposed a theory of multiple intelligence which includes intra-personal intelligence and interpersonal (social) intelligence.

- *Interpersonal Intelligence:* He conceptualized interpersonal intelligence as the ability to understand other people. What motivates them, how they work and how to work co-operatively with?
- *Intrapersonal Intelligence*: Is a correlative ability, turned inward. It is capacity to form an accurate vertical model of oneself and to be able to use that model to operate effectively in life.

Salovey and Mayer (1990)

Who coined the very term emotional intelligence; they described it as "a form of social intelligence that involves the ability to monitor one's own and others feelings and emotions, to discriminate among them and to use this information to guide one's thinking and actions." According to them, emotionally intelligent person is skilled in four areas-identifying, using, understanding and regulating emotions. This pioneering research was further enriched by contribution notably from Goleman (1995).

Goleman (1995)

According to him emotional intelligence consists of "abilities such as being able to motivate one and persist in the face of frustration, to control impulse and delay gratification, to regulate one's moods and keep distress from swamping the ability to think to empathize and to hope."

Golemam also stressed that emotional intelligence consists of five components:

1. Knowing one's emotions (Self-awareness).
2. Managing them (emotions).
3. Motivating self.
4. Recognizing emotions in others (empathy).
5. Handling relationships.

Goleman (1998)

Considered family and school are the places which can develop emotional and social competence *i.e.*, emotional intelligence.

He ascertained reviewing hundreds of studies that how parents treat their children whether with harsh discipline or empathic understanding, with indifference or warmth and so on has deep and lasting effect on the child's emotional life.

Gender Difference and Emotional Intelligence

Brackett and Mayer (2003)

There is considerable body of research an emotional intelligence and gender differences. Women have scored higher than men in emotional intelligence across the studies (Mayeret *et al*. 2002; Schutte, Mubuff, Hall, Haggetry, Cooper, Golden and Dornnheim, 1998; Thingujam and Ram, 2000).

Schutte et al. (1998); Furnham, (2000)

Did not find a significant gender difference in overall trait emotional intelligence.

Abraham Maslow, "If you always do what you have always done, you will always get what you have always got."

The Concept of Adjustment

The concept of adjustment is as old as human race on earth. The process of adjustment starts from the birth of child and continuous till his death. Psychologists use term 'adjustment' varying conditions of social or interpersonal relationship in the society. Adjustment means reaction to the demands and pressures of social environment imposed upon the individual. The demand may be external or internal to whom the individual to react (Agarwal 1996).

Origin of Adjustment

Herbert spencer introduced the term 'Adjustment' into scientific parlance in his principles of Biology in 1864. The meaning of adjustment was borrowed and changed from the concept of 'adaptation' in biology. Adaptation refers to the biological changes that facilitate the survival of a species. The process of adjustment starts from the birth of child and is continuous till his death. Psychologists use term 'adjustment' varying conditions of social or interpersonal relationship in the society. Adjustment means reaction to the demands and pressures of social environment imposed upon the individual. The demand may be external or internal to whom the individual is to react (Agarwal 1996).

Definitions of Adjustment

According to Carter V. Good (1959), "Adjustment is the process of finding and adopting modes of behaviour suitable to the environment or the changes in the environment".

Shaffer (1961) defined adjustment is the process by which a living organism maintains a balance between its needs and satisfaction of these needs.

Criteria of Good Adjustment

Any discussion of psychological adjustment carries with it judgments as to what constitutes good adjustment and what adjustments might be regarded as poor.

We may be inclined to regard well-adjusted people who are psychologically comfortable and who experience very little distress. Everyone at some time likely has experienced fear, anxiety and depression of mood unsolved or unsolvable problems. But good adjusted person copes well with his personal problems.

Norman Talent has suggested the following criteria of good adjustment.

(i) *Good Subjective Feeling:* A well adjusted person must be free from neurotic fears and anxiety and must feel psychologically comfortable. The individual sees meaning in his life.

(ii) *Personal and Social Achievement*: A maladjusted person should be able to develop his potentialities to the maximum. He or She should be able to achieve self-actualization. He or She should establish good relation in the society in conformity with the norms of the society.

(iii) *Ability to Work*: Adjustment refers to performance physical and mental work satisfactorily in accordance with one's capacity.

Areas of Adjustment

S. K. Mangal (1999) described main areas of adjustment:

1. *Home Adjustment:* Home is a source of greatest satisfaction and security of its members. The relationships among the family members and their ways of behaviour play a leading role in the adjustment of a child. All problematic and delinquent behaviours are the results of that adjustment and just maladjustment to a great extent, is the product of faulty rearing and uncongenial atmosphere at home.

   One should feel comfort and satisfaction in one's home in the spirit of 'Sweet Home'. He must have proper cordial relationships and behavioural adjustment with the members of his family. When the home and family environment are quite co-operative and congenial, members of the family get proper opportunity for satisfaction of their needs. In such encouraging, loving and peaceful family environment help the adolescents for their home adjustment.

2. *Health Adjustment*: One is said to be adjusted with regard to one's health and physical development and abilities are in conformity with those of his age-mates and he does not feel any difficulty in his progress due to some defects or in capabilities in his physical organs and he enjoys full opportunity of being adjusted. Adjustment is a process that takes us to lead a happy and well-contented life. Adjustment helps us in keeping balance between our needs and the capacity to meet these needs.

3. *Social Adjustment*: This area of adjustment is related with one's adjustment to his social surroundings. Person should feel satisfied with what he or she gets from his social environment. Person's adjustment with his social set up, starts from his parents, home and family and extended to the neighborhood, state, country and whole world. It is essential for the well-fare of his own and the society.

   How far one is adjusted can be as certained by one's social development and adaptability to the social environment. Social adjustment requires the development of social qualities and virtues in an individual. It also requires that one should be social enough to live in harmony with one's social beings and feel responsibility and obligation towards one's fellow beings society and country.

4. *Emotional Adjustment:* Emotions play an important role in controlling and directing one's behaviour and providing a definite shape to his personality make-up. An individual who is capable of expressing his emotions in a proper way at a proper time may be termed as emotionally adjusted.

   Emotions play a leading role in one's adjustment to self and his environment. An individual is said to be emotionally adjusted if he is able to express his emotions in a proper way at a proper time. It requires one's balanced emotional development and proper training in the outlet of emotions.

The Concept of Adolescents

In the development process of child a majority of parents feel that the youth years are the most difficult ones for child rearing. Youth is a period of physical and psychological maturity, when an individual is expected to establish his or her own identity responsible behaviour.

Erikson (1968) The youth's transition to adulthood can be a smooth process facilitated by the guidance of securing, nurturing and understanding parents in an emotionally conductive environment.

Goleman – (1995) A family where emotional bonding and communication between youth and parents are adequate with clear behavioural standards then youth can become emotionally competent, responsible, independent, confident and socially competent.

Erickson (1968) Adolescents as a good have long been regarded searching for themselves to find some form of indentify and meaning in their lives.

The Gale encyclopedic of childhood and adolescence sometimes referred to as teenage years, youth puberty, adolescence covers the period from roughly as 10 to 20 in a child's development.

The word adolescence is Latin in origin, derived from the verb adolescent, which means 'to grow into adulthood.' In all societies, adolescence is a time of growing up, of moving from the immaturity of childhood into the maturity of adulthood.

Puberty

The biological transition of adolescence, or puberty, is perhaps the most salient sign that adolescence has begun. Technically puberty refers to the period during which an individual becomes capable of sexual reproduction. Word puberty is used as a collective term to refer to all the physical changes that occur in the growing girl or boy as the individual passes from childhood into adulthood.

The physical changes of puberty are triggered by hormones, chemical substances in the body that act on specific organs and tissues. In boys a major change is the increased production of testosterone, a male sex hormone, while girls experience increased production of the female hormone estrogen.

Internally, through the development of primary sexual characteristics, adolescents become capable of sexual reproduction. Externally, as secondary sexual characteristics appear, girls and boys begin to look like mature women and men.

An adolescent is a person in the developmental stage, which spans from puberty up to and including adulthood. As far as age is concerned, adolescence occurs, in the case of girls, approximately between the ages of 12 and 18 years and is boys between 13 and 21 years of age.

Justification of the Study

Life in general and for a student in particular has become highly competitive. Almost all the attractive courses like medicine engineering agriculture etc., have competitive tests for admission. Due to high parental expectation, societal demands academic stress, anxiety of social approval, rising level aspiration adolescent group is becoming highly vulnerable.

Healthy family relations and academic climate help the students to do well in various walks of life and different kinds of competitive examinations emotional intelligence and adjustment helps the students to success in various fields and personal life.

In this scenario, it is intended to find out how family relationship and school climate affect on emotional intelligence and adjustment of adolescents.

The study has implications for counseling to adolescents. Poor family relationship and academic climate may be due to low emotional intelligence and adjustment of adolescents. Early detection of these relations in essential to make awareness in parents, teachers, school management and students. It can help the adolescents to cope better and handle more serious problems like suicide.

This research will be helpful at national and international level to understand how family relationship and academic climate play the role in developing children's emotional intelligence and adjustment. It is also helpful to educators, experts, psychologists and counselors to understand the student's psychological problems.

This research will be helpful to Government for planning curriculum and training programmes for teachers, students and parents EI training increaser learning, improves classrooms relationships and family relationships.

With the help of this study it could be possible to find out important emotional qualities required for successful students.

Summary

The concept of family relationship, types of parent-child relationship and parental attitude, concept of academic climate, concept of emotional intelligence and adjustment of adolescents was identified in this chapter. This chapter also presented the statement of problem and justification of the study.

2

REVIEW OF LITERATURE

Overview

Scientific literature helps the researcher in developing insight in the subject being studied. Review of literature helps in designing the study and also in finalizing the methodology of collecting reliable data. It provides a good outline for carrying for the study and also the gaps remained in the study.

Family Relationship and Emotional Intelligence

Family is the environment where the child learns to use their faculties and understand and cope with the physical world. It is a place where child learns how family relationships work, by observing their parents, siblings and other family members deal with each other. In joint families elder kinds assist their parents in bringing up of their younger brothers and sisters, which helps to develop responsibility, kindness, tolerance, sympathy, ability to consider needs of their family members and respectful attitude to others.

The family provides the first context for recognition and communication of affective massages to develop social intelligence and social competence of children. Children who reported that their parents modeled, encouraged, facilitated and rewarded emotional intelligent related behaviour enjoyed higher degree of emotional intelligence.

Fields and Casper (2001) stated, the family is defined in censuses and surveys as two or more persons related by blood, marriage or adoption and living in the same residence.

Martinez-Pons (1999) investigated adolescence perceptions of their parents parenting practices and their influence on their emotional intelligence. He found that children, who reported that their parents modeled, encouraged, facilitated and rewarded emotional intelligent related behaviour enjoyed higher degrees of emotional intelligence.

Ara (1986) found that parent-child relationships and parents personality was strongly associated with their adolescent children's personality.

Crosnoe, *et al*. (2002) examined, positive relationship between parents and their children can help to protect youth from engaging risky behaviour. Parents who are emotionally supportive and warm with their children they are less likely to use substance as such as alcohol or marijuana or engage in delinquent behaviour.

Begley and Schaefer, (1960) concluded that, few researchers also study the role of mother and reports that warm and affection of mothering is positively related to claim, happy and co-operative behaviour of children.

Cabrera *et al*. (2000) reported, father's today are often directly involved in rearing in numerous was, including and care giving-engaging in leisure and play activities, providing the child's mother with emotional and practical support and moral guidance and discipline.

Charlson (2006) examined, the biological father leaving away is associated with a greater risk of adverse child and adolescent outcomes whereas father living with children and involvement does not affect boys and girls differently but is more beneficial to the adolescent behavioural outcomes.

Hoffman, (1960) reported that, healthy father-child relationship leads to the feeling of being loved and accepted with a high degree of self-confidence and non-dependency.

Jossey Bass, (2009), stated young adults should learn to deal with their expending social universe and necessarily attain certain degree of emotional maturity to ward off deviances, as this period is also characterized by increased involvement of health risk behaviours.

Lamb (2004) stated, fathers high quality involvement is beneficial to children's well-being and development.

Mehat (1995) examined, parent-child sharing healthy and warm relationships was formed to develop social and emotional potentialities and get an advantage of getting parental suggestions.

Mithas, (1997) reported, emotional Competence was found to be greater in those early adolescents whose perceived mothering was associated with acceptance that of rejection.

Mayer, Dioaolo and Salovey (1990) Stated that emotionally intelligence person have been described as well adjusted warm, genuine, persistent and optimistic.

Sharpiro (2000) stated, children of democratic parents are generally observed to be sensitive to themselves and the environment, have high social skills have high self-esteem that is having high emotional intelligence.

Sim (2003) Reviewed earlier studies on father-adolescent relationship is characterized by physical and emotional distance; in contrast, the mother-adolescent relationship is characterized by attachment and intimacy.

Umadevi and Rayal (2004) stated, the emotional intelligence of the child depends on parental love and affection and depending on the child rearing practices interactions with them.

Warhol (1998) stated, the family environments where children first feel observe and learn about emotional relations. Therefore, a secure commitment between parents and children is expected especially in their early years. It had been observed that the stronger the emotional attachment between children and their family, the fewer emotional problems in later life. These children are also able to solve problems more easily.

Chopra, Rita and Nangru, Poonam (2013), examined that family relationship of high school students in relation to their emotional intelligence. 300 9th grade students were selected randomly from four DAV schools of Haryana. In the present study students perception of parental attitude *viz*; parental acceptance, parental concentration and parental avoidance in relation to their emotional intelligence was studied. Results of the study indicated that parental acceptance has significantly relationship with emotional intelligence whereas parental concentration has no significant relationship with emotional intelligence and parental avoidance has negative but significant relationship with emotional intelligence.

Dasgupta and Mukharjee (2011) examined, emotional intelligence as a mediator of work family role conflict, quality of life and happiness.

Bhatia Gunjan (2012) examined, the emotional intelligence of the students in relation to their family relationship. It attempts to show the effect of family relationship on the emotional intelligence of the adolescents. Emotional intelligence is defined in the terms of self-awareness, empathy, self-motivation, emotional stability, managing relations, integrity, self-development, value orientation, commitment, and altruistic behaviour and family relationship defined in terms of parental attitude acceptance, concentration and avoidance. The findings reveal that healthy family relationship greatly influences emotional intelligence of the adolescents. Family is the environment where the children learned to use their faculties and understand and cope with the physical world. It is a time when they don't bother with trivial things, such as the family relationship, because they know they are the kingpin of their family. It is the place, where they learn how family relationships work, by observing their parents, grandparents, siblings and rest of the family members deal with each other. They enjoy meeting them on family vacations and family reunions and exchanging Family reunion with them.

Morris *et al*. (2007) reported that family environment affects children's emotional intelligence in three aspects. *Firstly,* children learn emotions by observing the people around therm. *Secondly* their experiences and behaviours related to parent's emotions ensure children to become appropriate to society's expectations. *Thirdly* factors reflecting the emotional status of family such as the quality of emotional attachment between the child and the parents, attitude of parents, emotional and social openness, and marital relationship have impacts on emotional intelligence.

Alegre (2011) reported four main dimensions of parenting are identified that are relevant to the study of emotional intelligence, parental responsiveness, parental positive demandingness, parental negative demandingness, and parental emotion related coaching. Parental responsiveness, parental emotion related coaching, and parental positive demadingness are related to children's higher emotional intelligence, while parental negative demandingness is related to children's lower emotional intelligence.

Thompson (1998) indicates that children, who have positive relations with parents and argue the emotions of others, have a better understanding of emotions when compared with others. Children learn emotions from their parents' speeches and enhance their emotional intelligence through the bond they attached with their parents.

Alegre (2011) reported that due to the attitudes of parents have direct effects on children's emotional intelligence, it should be accepted that the enhancement of the parents' attitudes would be the first step to support emotional intelligence of children. While parents' attitudes are supported, children's emotional intelligence and home atmosphere are supported as well. Especially in early childhood it will be more effective to support parents' attitude to improve emotional intelligence of children.

Academic Climate and Emotional Intelligence

School is the major socialization institution for any child. School is one of the most important foundation pillars on which the child's personality develops. Children learn proficiencies in various abilities like learning processes and home work, social communications, handling emotions and the management of day-to-day interactions at home and schools. Academic climate is based on patterns of students, parents and school personnel's experience of school life and reflects norms, goals, values, interpersonal relationships, teaching and learning practices and organizational structure. All these factors of academic climate affect emotional intelligence of children.

Chen (2005) Brock, Nishidk, Choing, Grimm, Rimm Kaufman (2008) reported, school is a place where students get together share instructions and social infrastructures, which is fundamental to shaping their interests, attitudes and habits. Many activities in the classroom have an influence on the student's personality. School climate is an important input for building the healthy learning environment. A stimulating educational environment responsive to the needs of the individual can result in positive motivational consequences. On the contrary negative motivational consequences will result if the environment is not facilitative.

Schools climate refers to the quality and charter of school life. School climate is based on patterns of students, parents and school personnel's experience of school life and reflects norms, goals, values, interpersonal relationships, teaching and learning practices and organizational structures.

Hapin and Croft (1963) initiated a tradition of systematically studying the impact of school climate on student's learning and development. Early systematic studies of school climate were also spurred by organizational research as well as studies in school effectiveness. These studies tended to focus on observed characteristics.

Over the last three decades there has been an extra-ordinary growing body of research that attests to the importance of school climate. Positive school climate supports learning and positive youth development.

Finnegan (1996) argued that schools help students to learn the abilities underlying the emotional intelligence.

Abisamra (2000) reported that there is a positive relationship between emotional intelligence and academic achievement. He, therefore, canvassed for inclusion of EI in the schools' curricula.

McEvoy and Welker (2000) mentioned that positive interpersonal relationships and optimal learning opportunities for students in all demographic environments can increase achievement levels and reduce maladaptive behaviour. Schools climate can play a significant role in providing a healthy and positive school atmosphere.

Manning and Saddlemire (1996) conclude aspects of school climate, including trust, respect, mutual obligation and concern for others welfare can have powerful effects on educator's and learners' interpersonal relationships as well as learns academic achievement and over all school progress.

Rimm, Kaufaman (2007) Improving student's relationship with teachers has an important positive and long lasting implications for student's academic and social development. Those students who have close, positive and supportive relationships with their teachers will attain higher levels of achievement than those students with more unhealthy relationship. If a student feels personal connection to a teacher and receives more guidance and praise from the teachers, the student show more engagement in the academic content presented, display better classroom behaviour and achieve at higher levels academically. Teacher who fosters positive relationships with their students creates classroom environment more conducive to learning and meet students' developmental, emotional and academic needs.

Safavi *et al*. (2008) investigated the relationship between emotional intelligence and socio-emotional adjustment in pre-university girl students in Tehran. The results of the study showed that there a significant correlation between intelligence and socio-emotional adjustment.

Family Relationship and Adjustment

Adjustment if the process of finding and adopting modes of behaviour suitable to the environment or the changes of environment (Good, 1959). The home environment and parental involvement greatly contribute towards a child's developing and learning. When healthy relationship with parents in family prevails, the adolescent feels secure, well-adjusted and thinks himself accepted in family. Well adjusted person copes well with his personal problems. Family relationship particularly, parent's acceptance, concentrating or avoidance attitude affects adjustment of adolescents.

Shashidhar, S., Rao, C., Hegade, R. (2009) compared the scholastic performance of the children from corporation schools and private schools. The findings revealed that there is significantly high percentage of the low achievers among the children from corporation schools, which is attributed to their poor study habits and lack of support from parents and teachers.

Adams and Bennion (1990) found that parental control, exercised in a supportive environment in widely recognized an a facilitators of social development in adolescent.

Badani and Goswami (1973) studied the social adjustment in relation to some organic and environmental variables. They found that comparatively the female groups were significantly socially better adjusted than the male. They also found, the students falling into various socio-economic strata did not differ significantly in their social adjustment.

Chakra and Prabha (2004) found, emotional and social adjustment of children who are loved, accepted, nurtured, trusted and who are definitely superior.

Deepshikha and Suman Bhanot (2009) Study revealed that family environment played significant role in social adjustment of adolescent girls. Among the eight family environment factors, acceptance and caring, active reaction, orientation and organization adversity and significantly affected the social adjustment of adolescent girls, while independence on the social adjustment of adolescent girls.

Doyle and Moretti (2000) identified conferrable evidence that secure attachment continues to contribute to adjustment in adolescence. For example, more positive attachment to parents among 15 years old has been found to be associated with fewer mental problems such as anxiety, depression, inattention and conduct problems.

Lopez (1991) examined about the patterns of family conflict and their relation to college student's adjustment in 122 male and 332 female students. In the results, females and students who reported high levels of marital conflict in their current family environments evidenced lower personal adjustment.

Nihara, Tomayasu and Oshi (1987) found, the relationship between affective and emotional aspects of parental behaviour and the child's emotional adjustment is family and culture specific.

Dembo, Smau and Savin (1987) found that good relations with parents tend to show better social adjustment, emotional adjustment and self-esteem development.

Gupta (1990) found that parental education positively influenced the social adjustment of adolescent girls.

Aditi Sharma (2013) study aims to find out how the family climate, relations with peers and adjustment with others influence the overall personality and well-being of adolescents. The sample of 100 adolescents (25 boys and 25 girls from Government schools and 25 boys and 25 girls from public schools) was taken who were the students of 11th and 12th standard from various streams and administered on the Dimensions of Friendship Scale (DFS) by Chandha and Chadha, Adjustment Inventory for School Students by Sinha and Singh and Family Climate Scale by Shah. Data interpretation of Government and public school students on the peer group relations shows that on the dimension of enjoyment, trust, mutual assistance, understanding and spontaneity the students of Government and public schools do not differ significantly but on the dimension of acceptance and confiding they show significant difference. No significant difference is seen on the adjustment dimension. On the family climate variable significant difference is seen. Family climate of public school students is better than government school students.

Anita Sharma, Karuna and Jyoti Sharma (2013) study aimed to investigate the relationship between family environment and adjustment (home, health, social, emotional) in adolescents. The adolescents (100 males and 100 females) were assessed by using the Moos and Moos Family Environment Scale and Bells Adjustment Inventory. Family environment appeared to influence the adjustment of the adolescents. Data was analyzed in terms of Correlation, Regression Analysis and t-test. Regression Analysis revealed that family environment has explained 80 per cent of variance in gender (Males 32% Females 48%) and 92 per cent of variance in schools (government schools 18% and private schools 74%). t-test reveals that gender wise females have shown better adjustment than males and school wise private school students have shown better adjustment than government school students. Thus, it can be concluded that family environment plays a vital role in the adjustment of the adolescents.

Academic Climate and Adjustment

Various studies show that academic climate can affect many areas of adjustment and people within schools. For example a positive school climate has been associated with fewer behavioural and emotional problems of students (Kuperminc *et al*, 1997). School climate research suggests that positive interpersonal relationships and optimal learning opportunities for students in all demographic environments can increase achievement levels and reduce maladaptive behaviour (McEvoy and Welkar, 2000). In one study, high quality teacher students relationships appeared to be better predictors of classroom adjustment, social skills and reading performance for children showing initial externalizing, internalizing and learning problems than for children without these initial risk factors (Baker, 2006).

Way N., Reddy R. and Rhodes, J (2007) reported that, a cross-domain latent growth curve model was used to examine the trajectories of change in student perceptions of four critical dimensions of school climate (*i.e.,* teacher support, peer support, student autonomy in the classroom, and clarity and consistency in school rules and regulations) among 1,451 early adolescents from the beginning of sixth through the end of eight grade; and the effects of such trajectories on the rate of change in psychological and behavioural adjustment. Findings indicated that all the dimensions of perceived school climate declined over the 3 years of middle school. Furthermore, declines in each of the dimensions of perceived school climate were associated with declines over time in psychological and behavioural adjustment. Moreover, the direction of effects between each dimension of perceived school climate and psychological or behavioural adjustment were often unidirectional rather than bi-directional, underscoring the role of perceived school climate in the psychological and behavioural health of early adolescents. Gender and socio-economic class differences in these patterns are noted.

Raju, M. V. R and T. Khaja Rahamtulla (2007) stated the major findings of the study that adjustment of school children is primarily dependent on the school variables like the class in which they are studying and the type of management of the school.

Good (1959) Stated that adjustment is the process of finding and adopting modes of behaviour suitable to the environment or the changes in the environment.

Kulshresthe (1979) explained that adjustment process is a way in which the individual attempts to deal with stress, tensions, conflicts etc., and meet his or her needs. In this process the individual also makes efforts to maintain harmonious relationship with the environment.

Hayens and Comer (1993) found that a positive, supportive and culturally conscious school climate can significantly shape the degree of academic success experienced by urban students.

Freiberg (1998) Suggested that a positive school climate can yield positive educational and psychological outcomes for students and school personnel.

Battistich, Schaps and Willson (2004) found, positive Teacher – Student relationships evidenced by teacher's reports of low conflicts a high degree of closeness and support and little dependency – have been shown to support student's adjustment to school, contribute to their social skills, promote academic performance and foster students resiliency in academic performance.

Klem and Connell (2004) examined, eachers who experience close relationship with students reported that their students were less likely to avoid school, appeared self, directed, more co-operative and more engaged in learning.

Agarwal (1983) Stated that adjustment of principals was found to be a powerful prediction and their administrative effectiveness. Adjustment of principals to the teachers was not found to be significant related to their administrative effectiveness.

Devi (1979) found that physical education played a very important part in the adjustment of the adolescent girls.

Donga (1987) found that female trainees were more adjusted than male trainees.

Gupate (1990) found that adolescent girls studying in private schools showed significantly better social adjustment as compared to those of government schools.

Prasad (1985) found that primary and secondary teachers were almost similar in their total adjustment.

Gender, Residence, Emotional Intelligence and Adjustment

In this study Urban and Rural residence is considered. The urban and rural areas have their own distinctive features and they differ predominantly with each other in terms of homogeneity, integrity, occupations, environmental differences, social traditions, differences in size of communities, differences in physical facilities and educational level.

Urban and rural residence also differentiated on the basis of psychological attributes. For instance, the behaviour patterns, thoughts, beliefs and ideologies, patterns of socialization, social cohesion, emotional bonding, simplify and sincerity of relationships. Urban life is fast and stressful as compared to rural life. Those adolescents residing urban or rural areas are socialized and natured totally different situations. So it is expected that urban and rural situation can affect adolescent's emotional intelligence and various areas of adjustment.

Brackett and Mayer (2003) mentioned that, there is a considerable body of research an emotional intelligence and gender differences. Women have scored higher than men in emotional intelligence across the studies.

Schutte *et al*. (1998); Furnham (2000) they did not found significant gender difference in overall trait emotional intelligence.

Chadda (1985) found that no difference was observed between the emotional adjustment scores of various sub groups of teachers, *viz;* male female, rural and urban.

Chu (20002) revealed that males have higher level of emotional intelligence that the females. With regard to gender wise differences in adolescents, results are in contradiction with the findings of Abdullah and Maria (2008) who suggested that male students' overall level of adjustment was found to be as compared to female students.

Gupta (1990) found that, adolescent girls studying in urban schools were significantly better in their social adjustment as compared to girls in rural schools.

Gupta, Sushma (1990) found that parents of girls studying in urban and English medium schools had a better opinion regarding the social adjustment of their daughter as compared to the parents of girls in rural and Hindi medium schools adolescent girls studying in urban schools were significantly better in their social adjustment as compared to girls in rural schools.

Kaur (2007) stated that males were high on home, health, social and total adjustment.

Kumari (1988) found that sports girls belonging rural and urban areas were better in emotional social and educational adjustment than non sport girls.

Leong *et al*. (1990) investigated the cross cultural variations in stress and adjustment among 75 Asian and 129 Caucasion graduate students. Asian students reported experiencing fewer stressful life events, chronic health problems and total physical health problems than Caucasion students.

Nomani, H. R. (1965) found that no significant difference in the adjustment of males and females.

Pandey (1979) found that among students of higher secondary stage, the rural group to be better in emotional, health and school adjustment where as the urban group to be better in aesthetic adjustment significant relationship exists among adjustment, aspiration and achievement.

Prasad (1985) found that adjustment of teachers was related to their sex and with the level of their schools; males adjusted better than females.

Rather (1990) found that boys well as girls differed significantly in their adjustment. Boys showed more adjustment differentials in comparison to girls. Girls were found socially better adjusted than boys.

Sabh and Jangaiah (2005) found that no significant difference between male and female teachers in their adjustment.

Shah (1989) found that family climate was found to be effective in case of urban boys in determining their level of home adjustment. In case of girls, there was no relationship between family climate and home adjustment.

Shah (1989) found that urban boys had better adjustment than their rural counterparts; better home adjustment of adolescent was due to satisfactory family climate.

Shahpur (2004) reported that boys and girls do not difference in their adjustment.

Singh (2002) found females have higher emotional intelligence than the males.

Surekha (2008) found that student of private schools had better adjustment than students of government schools.

Tripathi (1981) found that girls were comparatively more adjusted to the home area.

Vamadevappa (2005) found no significant difference between boys and girls in their adjustment and also in health and educational adjustment areas; whereas significant difference was found in their home, social and emotional and adjustment; boys have better social and emotional adjustment than girls, but the girls have better home adjustment than boys.

Wing and Love (2001) reported that urban adolescents had comparatively better emotional intelligence and adjustment against rural counterparts. Female displayed higher emotional intelligence and better adjustment against their counterparts.

Richa Shukla and Dinesh Nagar (2013) reported emotional intelligence in the workplace is being recognized as an influential factor in enhancing the well being and work related outcomes. Similarly job performance is the most extensively researched criterion variable in both organizational bahaviour and human resource management literatures. The present study was conducted as part of a larger study in a public sector organization with an all India presence. This study explored the impact of gender and managerial levels on emotional intelligence and job performance. 300 IRS officers (232 Males and 68 Females) from the four zones (east, west, north and south) and three managerial levels (147 junior, 90 middle and 63 senior level) were asked to rate 60 items of emotional intelligence in a scale developed by Singh and 33 items in a self developed scale of job performance. Results found that female officers exhibit relatively higher social skills (component of EI) as compare to male officers whereas there is no difference in job performance among male and female officers. Furthermore, officers of senior managerial level exhibited higher self-regulation and social skills and also higher organizational commitment, satisfaction with rewards and incentives, high organizational support and total job performance as compared to the officers of junior and middle managerial levels.

Renuka Joshi and Manju Sharma (2013) an attempted to know the level of Emotional Intelligence among boys and girls. The data was collected on 180 subjects. ANOVA was used where 2 levels (Boys and Girls) were matched. Emotional Intelligence Scale was administered individually on all the subjects. Finding revealed that boys and girls differed significantly on Total Emotional Intelligence and its dimension namely: Self-Awareness, Self-Motivation, Emotional Stability, Self-Development, Value Orientation and Commitment from each other.

Alpana Vaidya (2013) reported that good health is the key to happiness and prosperity. It holds at any point in one's life time. The present paper is an attempt to study the relationship between quality of life and emotional intelligence among arts and commerce students in Pune city. The total sample consisted of 313 students from various colleges of Pune city where this course is taught. They were administered Quality of life scale and Emotional Intelligence scale. The quality of life was measured with the help of Comprehensive Quality of Life scale Adult (ComQol – A-5, 1997) developed by Robert Cummins. Emotional Intelligence was measured with the help of Schutte *et al*. (1998) scale. Data were analyzed using SPSS 18 for windows. Pearson's Product moment correlation was used to test the correlational hypotheses and Anova used to find out gender differences and faculty wise differences in quality of life and emotional intelligence. Results showed significant gender differences on Subjective Quality of Life (SQOL) but gender differences were not found on Objective Quality of Life (OQOL) and Emotional Intelligence (EI). Regarding faculty wise differences, obtained results showed that girls from arts faculty scored higher on SQOL.

Dheerja Singh School and Kiran Sahu (2013) reported that psychological well-being is a subjective term that means different things to different people. A positive state of mind engendering a sense of well-being that enables a person to function effectively within society and Emotional Intelligence is a type of Social Intelligence that involves the ability to monitor one's own and others emotions, to discriminating among them, and to use the information to guide one's thinking and action. The aim of the present study is to find out level of Psychological Well-Being and Emotional Intelligence among adolescent boys and girls and further to find out gender differences regarding these variables. For this purpose 150 adolescents (75 boys and 75 girls) of Moradabad district were taken, ranging from 13-17 years. To measure Emotional Intelligence Jyotsna Codaty's Emotional Intelligence Scale (2004) and to measure Psychological Well Being Warr's Psychological Well-Being scale were used in the present study; result indicated that these adolescents have higher level of psychological Well-Being while low level of Emotional Intelligence. Significant gender differences are found only for Emotional Intelligence. Further there is positive but non significant correlation between Psychological Well-Being and Emotional Intelligence.

Palak Malhotra and Kranti Sihotra (2013) reported that emotions play an important role in the life of an individual and one requires a higher emotional maturity to lead an effective life, especially the college students who are observed to be highly emotional in their dealings need to be studied. An emotionally mature person has the capacity to make effective adjustments with himself, members of his family, and his peers in the world, society and culture. As college students are the future and pillars of nation, so it is important to study their emotional maturity. Since college is a huge transition for freshers (first year students), it is a time for adjustment. The present study was undertaken to study the emotional maturity and adjustment level of college students. 52 boys and 52 girls within the age of 18 to 21 years from two Government colleges of Jammu were selected as a sample. Data was collected by administering Emotional Maturity scale by Singh and Bhargava. While adjustment inventory for college students (AICS) by Sinha and Singh was used to measure the adjustment level of college students. Normative survey method and Random sampling technique was used in the present study. The data obtained was analysed statistically and the study revealed that there is no significant difference in the emotional maturity and adjustment level of college going boys and girls.

Adsul, Ramesh K (2013) examined and compared the emotional intelligence and adjustment of urban and rural students. It was hypothesized that: *(i)* There would be significant difference between urban and rural students on four areas of emotional intelligence. *(ii)* There would be significant difference between urban and rural students on four areas of (home, health, social and emotional) adjustment. The 100 students (50 boys and 50 girls) studying in 11th class of various Junior colleges in Sangli district of Maharashtra State, India were selected by random sampling method. Study was conducted by using two psychological tests namely: *(i)* Mangal Emotional Intelligence Inventory. *(ii)* Bell's Adjustment Inventory. Mean, SD and 't'-test was used to analyze the data. The results of the study indicate that: 1. There were significant difference between urban and rural students on the different areas of emotional intelligence. The 't'-ratios of intra-personal awareness 3.06 ($p<.01$), inter-personal awareness 2.96 ($p<.01$), intra-personal management 2.22 ($p<.05$) , inter-personal management 1.22 (NS). It means that urban students have better emotional intelligence than rural students.(2) There were significant difference between urban and rural students on the different areas of adjustment. The 't' ratios of home 2.34 ($p<.05$), health 2.84 ($p<.01$), social 1.20 (NS), emotional 3.78 ($p<.01$). It means that urban students have better adjustment than rural students.

Summary

This chapter included research conducted on family relationship, academic climate, emotional intelligence and various areas of adjustments. These reviews showed various tools and techniques used by researchers to study these variables. It is observed that very few studies have been conducted on academic climate.

3

METHODOLOGY

Introduction

Emotional Intelligence and adjustment were important in older days, they are important today and in future also their significance will remain as it is. Though extensive work has been done regarding the correlate of emotional intelligence and adjustment, there is a dearth of studies presenting a complete and comprehensive picture of emotional intelligence and adjustment and its relevant variables. The purpose of study is to find out the effect of family relationship and academic climate on emotional intelligence and adjustment of adolescents.

Methodology is a very important part of any scientific research. This topic includes operational definitions of the variables, design of the study, aims, objectives and hypotheses of the study. It is also included standardized tools used for data collection and procedure of data collection.

Aim of the Study

Family and school is an undivided part of every student's life. Most of their time, they spend in school and family. School and teacher teaches him, how to live in the competitive life with well adjustment by knowing own motives, and emotions. Hence the main aim of the study was to find out the effect of family relationship, and academic climate on emotional intelligence and adjustment of adolescents.

Objectives of the Study

Some major objectives were kept for present research works as under.

1. To find out the difference between male and female adolescents on their mothers and fathers acceptance, concentration and avoidance attitude.
2. To search the difference between male and female adolescents perception on various components of academic climate.
3. To investigate the difference between male and female adolescents on various dimensions of emotional intelligence.
4. To search the difference between male and female adolescents on various areas of adjustment.
5. To find out the difference between urban and rural adolescents perception on their mothers and fathers acceptance, concentration and avoidance attitude.
6. To search the difference between urban and rural adolescents perception on their various dimensions of academic climate.
7. To find out the difference between urban and rural adolescents on various dimensions of emotional intelligence.
8. To examine the difference between urban and rural adolescents on various areas of adjustment.
9. To search the effects of various levels of parental acceptance, concentration and avoidance attitude on emotional intelligence of adolescents.
10. To examine the effect of various dimensions of academic climate on emotional intelligence of adolescents.
11. To find out the effect of various levels of parental acceptance, concentration and avoidance attitude on adjustment of adolescents.
12. To search the effect of various dimensions of academic climate on adjustment of adolescents.

13. To study the main and interaction effect of family relationship (parents acceptance attitude towards their child) and academic climate on emotional intelligence.
14. To investigate the main and interaction effect of family relationship (concentration) and academic climate on emotional intelligence of adolescents.
15. To see the main and interaction effect of family relationship (avoidance attitudes) and academic climate on emotional intelligence of adolescents.
16. To explore the main and interaction influence of family relationship (acceptance attitudes) and academic climate on adjustment of adolescents.
17. To search the main and interaction impact of family relationship (concentration attitudes) and academic climate on adjustment of adolescents.
18. To investigate the main and interaction effect of family relationship (avoidance attitude) and academic climate on adjustment of adolescents.

Hypotheses of the Study

Following hypotheses were tested in the study.

1. Male and Female adolescents would not differ on their mothers and fathers acceptance attitude.
2. There will be no significant difference between male and female adolescents on their mothers and fathers concentration attitude.
3. There would be no significant difference between male and female adolescents on their mothers and fathers avoidance attitude.
4. There would be no significant difference between male and female adolescents perception on various components of academic climate.
5. There will be no significant difference between male and female adolescents on various dimensions of emotional intelligence.

6. There will be no significant difference between male and female adolescents on various areas of adjustment.
7. There will be no significant difference between urban and rural adolescents on their mothers and fathers acceptance attitude.
8. There will be no significant difference between urban and rural adolescents on their mothers and fathers concentration attitude.
9. There will be no significant difference between urban and rural adolescents on their mothers and fathers avoidance attitude.
10. There would be no significant difference between urban and rural adolescents perception on their various dimensions of academic climate.
11. There will be no significant difference between urban and rural adolescents on various dimensions of emotional intelligence.
12. There will be no significant difference between urban and rural adolescents on various areas of adjustment.
13. The various levels of parental acceptance will yield different outcomes of emotional intelligence of adolescents.
14. There is no significant effect on adjustment of various levels of parental acceptance of adolescents.
15. There exists no significant effect of levels of parental concentration on emotional intelligence of adolescents.
16. There exists no significant effect of various levels of parental concentration on adjustment of adolescents.
17. There exists no significant effect of various levels of parental avoidance attitude on emotional intelligence and its four dimensions.
18. There exists no significant effect of various levels of parental avoidance on adjustment and its four areas.
19. There exists no significant effect of various levels of physical material (a dimension of academic climate) on emotional intelligence.

20. There exists no significant effect of various levels of physical material (a dimension of academic climate) on adjustment.
21. There exists no significant effect of various levels of Inter personal Trust (a dimension of academic climate) on emotional intelligence.
22. There exists no significant effect of various levels of Inter personal Trust (a dimension of academic climate) on adjustment.
23. There exists no significant effect of various levels of School Provisions (a dimension of academic climate) on emotional intelligence.
24. There exists no significant effect of various levels of school provisions (a dimension of academic climate) on adjustment.
25. There exists no significant effect of various levels of academic provisions (a dimensions of academic climate) on emotional intelligence.
26. There exists no significant effect of various levels of academic provisions (a dimensions of academic climate) on adjustment.
27. There exists no significant effect of various levels of academic climate on emotional intelligence.
28. There exists no significant effect of various levels of academic climate on adjustment.
29. Parental acceptance attitude and academic climate will be jointly and significantly interact to yield different outcomes of emotional intelligence.
30. Parental concentration attitude and academic climate will jointly and significantly interact to yield different outcomes of emotional intelligence.
31. Parental avoidance attitude and academic climate will jointly and significantly interact to yield different outcomes of emotional intelligence.

32. Parental acceptance attitude and academic climate will jointly and significantly interact to yield different outcomes of adjustment.
33. Parental concentration attitude and academic climate will jointly and significantly interact to yield different outcomes of adjustment.
34. Parental avoidance attitude and academic climate will jointly and significantly interact to yield different outcomes of adjustment.

Operational Definitions of Variables

Gender and area of residence are considered as demographic variables whereas family relationship, academic climate, emotional intelligence and adjustment are considered as major variables of the study. The operational definitions of the major variables are as under:

Family Relationship

Family Relationship means adolescents' perceived their parental attitude of acceptance, concentration and avoidance as measured by family relationship inventory.

Academic Climate

Academic Climate means adolescents' perception of their school climate on various dimensions like physical material, interpersonal trust, school provisions and academic provisions, which is measured by academic climate description questionnaire.

Emotional Intelligence

Emotional Intelligence is the ability to identify, use, understand and manage emotions in positive ways to relieve stress and communicate effectively, which is measured by emotional intelligence scale.

Adjustment

Adjustment means the reaction to the demands and pressures of social environment imposed upon the adolescents. The demand may be external or internal. Adjustment in various areas measured by adjustment inventory.

Design of the Study

For the present study 3x3 factorial research design has been employed. Family relationship and academic climate were independent variables while emotional intelligence and adjustment were dependent variables. Three levels of each independent variables *viz.,* high, average and low has been considered for present study.

Method

Sample

Present research has been conducted in three districts of Western Maharashtra *viz;* Sangli, Satara and Kolhapur. 847 students of 11th class has been selected by random sampling method for this research. The ratio of the sample among these three districts was kept as 1:1:1. Students studying in 11th class were selected on the basis of gender and residence. The ratio of these two criteria was 1:1 and the varied in age range from 16 to 17 years. 30 Junior colleges among Sangli, Satara and Kolhapur districts have been visited to collect the sample students.

Table 3.1: Demographic Characteristics of the Study Sample

Districts	N	Urban		Rural	
		Male	Female	Male	Female
Sangli	282	70	73	75	64
Satara	282	65	73	75	69
Kolhapur	283	65	73	77	68
Total	**847**	**200**	**219**	**227**	**201**

Tools used for Data Collection

For the present study four tools were used. Four tools were standardized psychological tests. The obtained demographic information regarding age, gender and area of residence were asked to fill up information on the front page of family relationship inventory. Detailed information about tools used for data collection is as under:

Family Relationship Inventory (FRI)

Family Relationship Inventory is prepared by Sherry and Sinha (1987) on the basis of Brunken and Crites's 'Family Relationship Inventory' in the Indian situations. An inventory may well discriminate the individuals who feel emotionally accepted, over protected or rejected by their parents. The inventory contains 150 items classified into three patterns of mother and father separately. Scoring Table 3.1 is given on the first page of the inventory. For every true responses one mark is to be given and marks obtained by the respondents are summed up area wise. A high score in each area of the inventory indicated a high degree of one's feelings of his being accepted, concentrated or avoided by his mother or father or both parents. Test-retest reliability and validity of inventory is moderately high.

Academic Climate Description Questionnaire (ACDQ)

This questionnaire is developed by Shah and Shah (1988). It consists 84 items. The scale have four dimensions with 16 items for physical material, 14 items for interpersonal trust, 32 items for school provisions and 22 items for academic provisions. The students are required to tick only one response of the three given alternatives for each item. It's scoring procedure is very simple. The responses are scored as follows:

(i) 2 for the positive statement [response alternative (A)].

(ii) 1 for the neutral statement [response alternative (B)].

(iii) 0 for negative statement [response alternative (C)].

Thus, the maximum score is 168 and the minimum is zero. High score indicates high academic climate while low score indicates low academic climate. Test has split half reliability value is 0.85 and test-retest reliability found 0.78. Test has high content validity.

Mangal Emotional Intelligence Inventory (MEII)

This inventory developed by S. K. Mangal and Shubhra Mangal (2004). The inventory has 100 items with 'Yes' or 'No' alternatives. This inventory has four aspects namely: *(i)* Intrapersonal awareness, *(ii)* Interpersonal awareness, *(iii)* Intrapersonal management and *(iv)* Interpersonal Management. It is forced choice inventory. The response 'Yes' is an indicator the presence of emotional intelligence and 'No' for the lack of emotional intelligence. There are some items of adverse meaning. Reliability measured by split-half, K-R formula and test-retest methods and found quiet high that in neat about 0.90. Validity assessed by factorial and criterion approach and found quiet high.

Bell's Adjustment Inventory

This inventory is developed by R. K. Ojha (1994). This inventory includes four parts: *(i)* Home, *(ii)* Health, *(iii)* Social and *(iv)* Emotional. Each part has 35 statement which are answered 'Yes' or 'No'. Scoring of inventory is most easy. The 'Yes' responses are counted. For each 'Yes' response 1 score is to be given. The total number of 'Yes' scores thus makes total score of the individual in the part. The inventory is totally negative inventory. When an individual answers in 'Yes', it indicates his difficulties. Reliability is measured by split-half and test-retest method and average of reliability on all dimensions are above 0.85 which is very high. Validity of this inventory is above 0.75. High score on this inventory denotes unsatisfactory adjustment while low score denotes excellent adjustment.

Procedure of Data Collection

For administering the psychological scales first permission of the heads of the Junior Colleges was sought. After completion of these formalities the selected subjects of that Jr. College were collected in a class room where 20 to 25 subjects could sit comfortably and sufficient distance could be kept between the two subjects. So that one could not see the responses written by other. Once the subjects seat comfortably, through informal talk, rapport formation was done. Once, it was found that the subjects are ready to take the psychological scale; first copies of 'Family Relationship Inventory' were distributed among them. The subjects were given standard instructions laid by inventory.

After completing 'Family Relationship Inventory' short rest of five minutes was given the subjects. After it, they were asked to start to respond second scale 'Academic Climate Description Questionnaire' (ACDQ). After completion of this scale subjects were given five minutes rest.

In the next session subjects were asked to respond third scale 'Mangle Emotional Intelligence Inventory'. After completion of this scale final scale copies of 'Bell's Adjustment Inventory' were distributed among the subjects. Similar procedure was adopted for collecting data from different groups of subjects.

Statistical Treatment of Data

Data analysis is carried out with the help of Statistical Package for the Social Sciences (SPSS). After collecting the data, all psychological scales were hand scored by the researcher.

First, the data were treated by mean, S.D. and 't' test. *Secondly* One Way ANOVA was used for examining, whether the groups differ significantly or not. Two Way ANOVA was used to see the main and interaction effects of independent variables. *Finally,* post-hock comparison was done to see the intergroup mean differences are significant or not.

STATISTICAL INTERPRETATION OF RESULTS

Introduction

Interpretation of results is decisive step in process of research. In this chapter interpretation of results has been attempted on the collected data. The collected data is analyzed by descriptive statistics, 't' test and analysis of variance (ANOVA). 3x3 factorial design has been applied. The main aim of the study was to search the effect of family relationship and academic climate on emotional intelligence and adjustment of adolescents. Regarding this view the result of Family Relationship Inventory (FRI), Academic Climate Descriptive Questionnaire (ACDQ), Mangal Emotional Intelligence Inventory (EMII) and Bell's Adjustment Inventory (BAI) scores are interpreted in present chapter.

Descriptive Statistics

Table 4.1: Showing the Descriptive Statistics Analysis of Major Variables

	Family Relationship				Academic Climate			
	1				2			
	PA	PC	PV	PM	IPT	SP	AP	Total AC
Mean	36.80	24.13	19.00	26.51	24.22	47.01	36.15	139.10
Median	38.00	24.00	17.00	27.00	25.00	49.00	38.00	143.00

Condt...

	1			2				
Mode	39.00	24.00	5.00	30.00	28.00	53.00	40.00	149.00
SD	6.40	5.41	11.72	4.58	4.76	8.55	6.69	17.11
Skewness	-0.53	0.18	0.86	-0.76	0.03	-1.16	-1.04	-1.09
Kurtosis	1.49	0.72	0.71	1.87	7.08	1.84	0.90	1.50
Minimum	9.00	6.00	00	3.00	2.00	6.00	10.00	63.00
Maximum	66.00	42.00	57.00	51.00	58.00	62.00	51.00	195.00
N	847	847	847	847	847	847	847	847

	Emotional Intelligence				
	Intra PA	Inter PA	Intra PM	Inter PM	Total EI
Mean	15.26	14.84	17.84	16.86	64.81
Median	15.00	15.00	18.00	17.00	65.00
Mode	14.00	15.00	19.00	17.00	74.00
SD	3.57	3.31	3.77	3.51	10.67
Skewness	-0.12	-0.25	-0.53	-0.18	-0.15
Kurtosis	-0.17	0.07	0.15	0.32	-0.61
Min.	4.00	2.00	00	6.00	31.00
Max.	24.00	23.00	29.00	33.00	90.00
N	847	847	847	847	847

	Adjustment				
	Home	Health	Social	Emotional	Total Adjustment
Mean	14.84	10.98	19.12	15.04	59.99
Median	15.00	10.00	19.00	16.00	60.00
Mode	18.00	10.00	19.00	20.00	70.00
SD	4.97	6.00	4.07	6.66	16.32
Skewness	0.32	0.50	0.04	-0.13	0.18
Kurtosis	-0.39	-0.34	0.97	-0.50	-0.39
Min.	3.00	00	4.00	00	20.00
Max.	29.00	30.00	35.00	36.00	118.00
N	847	847	847	847	847

Table 4.2: Mean, SD, Number, Gender and Residence of Adolescents on Family Relationship (Parental Attitudes)

Gender	Residence		Family Relationship		
			Acceptance	Concentration	Avoidance
Male	Urban	Mean	36.89	23.20	13.42
		SD	6.60	4.99	10.96
		N	200	200	200
	Rural	Mean	36.27	25.35	25.10
		SD	6.72	5.25	11.16
		N	227	2.27	227
	Total	Mean	36.56	24.34	21.03
		SD	6.67	5.23	11.87
		N	427	4.27	427
Female	Urban	Mean	37.36	23.99	15.50
		SD	6.00	5.51	10.89
		N	219	219	219
	Rural	Mean	36.72	23.84	18.50
		SD	6.23	5.67	11.37
		N	201	201	201
	Total	Mean	37.05	23.92	16.94
		SD	6.11	5.58	11.21
		N	4.20	4.20	420
Total	Urban	Mean	37.13	23.61	15.94
		SD	6.29	5.27	10.92
		N	4.19	419	419
	Rural	Mean	36.48	24.64	22.00
		SD	6.49	5.50	11.72
		N	428	428	428
	Total	Mean	36.80	24.13	19.00
		SD	6.40	5.41	11.72
		N	847	847	847

Table 4.3: Mean, SD, Number, Gender and Residence of Adolescents on Various Dimensions of Academic Climate

Gender	Residence		Academic Climate				
			Physical Material	Interpersonal Trust	School Provision	Academic Provision	Total AC
Male	Urban	Mean	25.73	23.86	46.78	35.66	139.02
		SD	4.19	4.16	8.40	5.85	17.58
		N	200	200	200	200	200
	Rural	Mean	25.12	23.29	44.33	32.32	132.75
		SD	4.87	6.00	9.34	7.65	18.77
		N	227	227	227	227	227
	Total	Mean	25.40	23.55	45.48	33.88	135.69
		SD	4.84	5.22	8.98	7.06	18.47
		N	427	427	427	427	427
Female	Urban	Mean	27.26	25.02	48.48	38.53	139.89
		SD	3.88	3.16	6.80	4.94	14.87
		N	219	219	219	219	219
	Rural	Mean	28.05	24.78	48.66	38.36	145.50
		SD	4.10	4.97	8.78	5.86	14.29
		N	201	201	201	201	201
	Total	Mean	27.64	24.90	48.56	38.45	142.57
		SD	4.00	4.13	7.80	5.39	14.85
		N	420	4.20	420	420	420
Total	Urban	Mean	26.52	24.47	47.67	37.16	139.47
		SD	4.40	3.71	7.64	5.58	16.21
		N	419	419	419	419	419
	Rural	Mean	26.50	23.99	46.36	35.16	138.74
		SD	4.75	5.59	9.32	7.49	17.96
		N	428	428	4.28	428	428
	Total	Mean	26.51	24.22	47.01	36.15	139.10
		SD	4.58	4.76	8.55	6.69	17.11
		N	847	847	847	847	847

Table 4.4: Mean, SD, Number, Gender and Residence of Adolescents on Various Dimensions of Emotional Intelligence

Gender 1	Residence 2		Emotional Intelligence 3				
			Intrapersonal Awareness	Interpersonal Awareness	Intrapersonal Management	Interpersonal Management	Total EI
Male	Urban	Mean	15.53	15.04	17.63	16.42	64.63
		SD	3.81	3.35	3.97	3.86	11.94
		N	200	200	200	200	200
	Rural	Mean	15.15	14.74	17.66	16.46	64.03
		SD	3.81	3.43	3.61	3.54	10.49
		N	227	227	227	227	227
	Total	Mean	15.33	14.88	17.64	16.44	64.31
		SD	3.81	3.39	3.78	3.69	11.19
		N	427	427	427	427	427
Female	Urban	Mean	15.32	14.86	18.01	17.17	65.38
		SD	3.22	3.15	3.59	3.32	9.72
		N	219	219	219	219	219
	Rural	Mean	15.03	14.74	18.06	17.41	65.27

Condt…

1	2		3				
		SD	3.42	3.33	396	3.21	10.55
		N	201	201	201	201	201
	Total	Mean	15.19	14.80	18.04	17.29	65.33
		SD	3.31	3.23	376	3.27	10.11
		N	420	420	420	420	420
Total	Urban	Mean	15.42	14.94	17.83	16.41	65.02
		SD	3.51	3.24	3.77	3.60	10.83
		N	419	419	419	419	419
	Rural	Mean	510	14.74	17.85	16.91	64.61
		SD	3.63	3.38	3.78	3.42	10.53
		N	428	428	428	428	428
	Total	Mean	15.26	14.84	17.84	16.86	64.81
		SD	3.57	3.31	3.77	3.51	10.67
		N	847	847	847	847	847

Table 4.5: Mean, SD, Number, Gender and Residence of Adolescents on Various Areas of Adjustment

Gender	Residence		Adjustment				
			Home	Health	Social	Emotional	Total Adjustment
Male	Urban	Mean	14.61	10.63	18.75	13.33	57.32
		SD	5.40	6.39	3.61	6.61	17.22
		N	200	200	200	200	200
	Rural	Mean	16.55	11.91	20.04	15.57	64.08
		SD	5.11	7.07	4.98	7.29	18.10
		N	227	227	227	227	227
	Total	Mean	15.64	11.31	19.43	14.52	60.91
		SD	5.33	6.78	4.44	7.06	18.00
		N	427	427	4.27	4.27	427
Female	Urban	Mean	14.17	10.50	18.85	15.25	58.78
		SD	4.78	5.04	3.50	6.15	14.42
		N	219	219	219	219	219
	Rural	Mean	13.86	10.82	18.74	15.95	59.35
		SD	4.07	5.11	3.81	6.22	14.36
		N	201	201	201	201	201
	Total	Mean	14.02	10.65	18.80	15.57	59.05
		SD	445	5.07	3.65	6.18	14.37
		N	420	420	420	420	420
Total	Urban	Mean	14.38	10.56	18.80	14.33	58.08
		SD	5.08	5.71	3.55	6.44	15.82
		N	419	419	419	419	419
	Rural	Mean	15.28	11.40	19.43	15.74	61.86
		SD	4.83	6.25	4.51	6.80	16.60
		N	428	428	428	428	428
	Total	Mean	14.84	10.98	19.12	15.04	59.99
		SD	4.97	6.00	4.07	6.66	16.32
		N	847	847	847	847	847

Before analyzing the data by various statistical techniques, it is essential to perform the descriptive statistics of raw scores detailed from the psychological tools. It is helpful for describe a large value of data with just a few values like: mean, median, mode, standard deviation, skewness and kurtosis.

Descriptive statistics values are shown in the Table 4.1.

At the beginning interpretation of results has been attempted by 't' test. The results present the analysis regarding the comparison of gender, area of residence on family relationship, academic climate, emotional intelligence and adjustment of adolescents. The 't' test of independent sample has been employed for comparison the groups. Hypothesis-wise interpretation is given below.

Hypothesis No. 1: Male and Female adolescents would not be differ on their mothers and fathers acceptance (PA) attitude.

Table 4.6: Showing the Mean, SD and 't' Value of Mothers and Fathers Acceptance Attitude of Male and Female Adolescents

	Sex	N	Mean	Std. Deviation	df	t
MA	Male	427	18.8899	4.01927		1.43
	Female	420	19.2673	3.59893	845	
FA	Male	427	17.7330	3.48490		.40
	Female	420	17.7232	3.66540		
PA	Male	427	36.5644	6.67012		1.09
	Female	420	37.0477	6.12139		

* = 0.05, ** = 0.01 significant level

Table 4.6 shows that the mean value of mother's acceptance attitude of male adolescents is 18.89 and SD value is 4.01. While female adolescents have 19.26 mean values and 3.59 SD. It is seen that there is a miner difference between these two means and it's 't' value is 1.43 which is not significant even 0.05 alpha level. It is also noticed that mean values of male and female adolescents on fathers acceptance attitude is 17.73 and 17.72 and their SD values are 3.48 and 3.66 respectively. There is no more difference between two means. Parental acceptance attitude 't' value is 1.09. So male and female adolescents are not significantly differ on parental acceptance attitude. Thus the null hypothesis 'male and female adolescents would not be differing on their mothers and fathers acceptance attitude strongly accepted in the present study.

Hypothesis No. 2: There will be no significant difference between male and female adolescents on their mothers and fathers concentration attitude.

Table 4.7: Showing the Mean, SD and 't' Values of Mothers and Fathers Concentration Attitude of Male and Female Adolescent

	Sex	N	Mean	Std. Deviation	Std. Error Mean	t
MC	Male	427	13.7400	3.19115	.15443	1.41
	Female	420	14.0477	3.11542	.15220	
FC	Male	427	10.6112	3.04869	.14754	3.15**
	Female	420	9.9117	3.38789	.16551	
PC	Male	427	24.3466	5.23950	.25356	1.18
	Female	420	23.9069	5.58608	.27290	

* = 0.05, ** = 0.01 significant level

Table 4.7 showing the mean and SD values of mothers concentration attitude of male and female adolescents. It is observed that mean value of male adolescents is 13.74 and SD value is 3.19, while female adolescents' mean is 14.07 and SD value is 3.11. There is a minor difference between these two means and it's 't' value is 1.41 which is not significant even 0.05 level. So there is no significant difference between male and female adolescents on their mother's concentration attitude. On the contrary male and female adolescents mean values on fathers' concentration attitude is 10.61, 9.91 and SD values 3.04, 3.38 respectively. There is difference between two means and its 't' value is 3.15. It is significant on 0.01 alpha level. It means that fathers are more concentrating on their male adolescents than female adolescents. So null hypothesis No. 2 is partly accepted.

Hypothesis No. 3: There would be no significant difference between male and female adolescents on their mothers and fathers avoidance attitude.

Table 4.8: Showing the Mean, SD and 't' Value of Mothers and Fathers Avoidance Attitude of Male and Female Adolescents

	Sex	N	Mean	Std. Deviation	Std. Error Mean	t
MV	Male	427	10.6347	6.61890	.32031	4.50**
	Female	420	8.6038	6.50768	.31792	
FV	Male	427	10.3536	5.82684	.28198	5.12**
	Female	420	8.3628	5.45378	.26643	
PV	Male	427	21.0351	11.87637	.57474	5.15**
	Female	420	16.9427	11.22994	.54862	

* = 0.05, ** = 0.01 significant level

Table 4.8 shows that the mean value of mother's avoidance attitude of male adolescents is 10.63 and female avoidance is 8.60. The SD values of male and female adolescents are 6.62 and 6.51 respectively. And it's 't' value is 4.50. This 't' value is significant on 0.01 level. The mean value of fathers avoidance attitude of male and female adolescents are 10.35 and 8.36 and SD values are 5.82 and 5.45 respectively and it's 't' value is 512. It is significant on 0.01 alpha level. These results indicate that there is a significant difference between male and female adolescents on their mothers and fathers avoidance attitude. Mothers and fathers have more avoidance attitude to males then females.

Hypothesis No. 4: There would be no significant difference between male and female adolescents perception on various components of academic climate.

Still gender is a most debatable issue in globalization era. It is always taking into consideration for gender difference by various scholars and investigators. In the present study such an attempt has been made and hypothesis were formulated 'there would be no significant difference between male and female adolescents on various dimensions of academic climate'. It is found that the perception of male and female adolescents is different regarding 'physical material of school.

Table 4.9: The Mean, SD and 't' Values of Various Dimensions of Academic Climate Perception of Male and Female Adolescents

Academic Climate	Sex	N	Mean	Std. Deviation	Std. Error Mean	t
PM	Male	427	25.4098	4.84048	.23425	7.34**
	Female	420	27.6539	4.00622	.19572	
IPT	Male	427	23.5597	5.22975	.25309	4.20**
	Female	420	24.9236	4.12530	.20153	
SP	Male	427	45.4848	8.98730	.43493	5.29**
	Female	420	48.5489	7.80561	.38133	
AP	Male	427	33.8899	7.06406	.34185	10.54**
	Female	420	38.4535	5.40553	.26408	
ACL Total	Male	427	135.6909	18.47567	.89410	5.96**
	Female	420	142.5704	14.86805	.72635	

* = 0.05, ** = 0.01 significant level

Dimensions of Academic climate PM = Physical Material, IPT = Interpersonal Trust, P = School Provisions, AP= Academic Provisions. Total ACL = Total Academic Climate

The mean value of male and female adolescents is 25.41 and 27.65 respectively and SD value is 4.84 and 4.00 respectively. The 't' value of this difference is 7.34 which is strongly significant on 0.01 level. It is also observed that male and female adolescents are significantly differ on 'interpersonal trust', school provisions', academic provisions' and 'total academic climate'. The 't' value of these dimensions are 7.34, 4.20, 5.29, 10.54 and 5.96. These values are significant on 0.01 alpha level. It is observed that female adolescent's perception of their academic climate is better than male adolescents. So null hypothesis is rejected.

Hypothesis No. 5: There will be no significant difference between male and female adolescents on various dimensions of emotional intelligence.

Table 4.10: Shows the Mean, SD and 't' Values of Various Dimensions of Emotional Intelligence of Male and Female Adolescents

Dimensions of Emotional Intelligence	Sex	N	Mean	Std. Deviation	Std. Error Mean	t
Intra PA	Male	427	15.3349	3.81654	.18470	.59
	Female	420	15.1909	3.32265	.16232	
Inter PA	Male	427	14.8852	3.39337	.16422	.30
	Female	420	14.8162	3.23662	.15812	
Intra PM	Male	427	17.6487	3.78324	.18308	1.50
	Female	420	18.0406	3.77232	.18429	
Inter PM	Male	427	16.4450	3.69477	.17880	3.51**
	Female	420	17.2888	3.27527	.16001	
EI	Male	427	64.3138	11.19062	.54155	1.39
	Female	420	65.3365	10.13185	.49497	

* = 0.05, ** = 0.01 significant level

Intra PA = Intrapersonal Awareness, Inter PA = Interpersonal Awareness, Intra PM = Intrapersonal Management, Inter PM = Interpersonal Management, EI = Emotional Intelligence.

Table 4.10 shows that the mean value of interpersonal awareness of male adolescents is 15.33 and SD value is 3.82. Similarly the mean value of female adolescents is 15.19 and SD is 3.32. It is not significant even 0.05 level. Other dimensions of emotional intelligence like 'interpersonal awareness' and 'interpersonal management' indicate no significant difference. However mean value of male adolescents on interpersonal management is 16.44 and SD is 3.69, similarly the mean value of female adolescents is 17.29 and SD is 3.27. It is significant at 0.01 level. It indicates that there is significant difference in male and female adolescents on interpersonal management. Female adolescents have more ability of interpersonal management than male adolescents. That's why this hypothesis is partly accepted.

Hypothesis No. 6: There will be no significant difference between male and female adolescents on various areas of adjustment.

Table 4.11: Showing the Mean, SD and 't' Value of Various Areas of Adjustment of Male and Female Adolescents

Areas of Adjustment	Sex	N	Mean	Std. Deviation	Std. Error Mean	t
Home	Male	427	15.6417	5.33176	.25802	4.81**
	Female	420	14.0143	4.45228	.21751	
Health	Male	427	11.3138	6.78889	.32854	1.67
	Female	420	10.6277	5.05092	.24675	
Social	Male	427	19.4379	4.44029	.21488	2.72**
	Female	420	18.8019	3.65647	.17863	
Emotional	Male	427	14.5246	7.06883	.34208	2.28*
	Female	420	15.5656	6.19479	.30264	
Overall Adjustment	Male	427	60.9180	18.00014	.87109	1.70
	Female	420	59.0095	14.35920	.70149	

* = 0.05, ** = 0.01 significant level

In connection with Table 4.11 adjustment of male and female adolescents. It is found that mean value of home adjustment of male adolescents is 15.64 and SD is 5.33 .Similarly the mean value of female adolescents is 14.01 and SD is 4.45. The calculated 't' value is 4.81. It is significant at 0.01 level. It indicates that there is significant difference between male and female adolescents on home adjustment. Regarding manual of adjustment less score indicates good adjustment. So it is interpreted that female adolescents have good home adjustment than male adolescents.

In health adjustment mean value of male adolescents is 11.31 and SD is 6.79. Similarly female adolescents mean value is 10.63 and SD is 5.05. The calculated 't' value is 1.67. It is not significant. There is no difference between male and female adolescent on health adjustment.

Regarding social adjustment male adolescents mean value is 19.43 and SD is 4.44. The mean value of female adolescents is 18.80 and SD is 3.66. The 't' value is 2.72. It is significant at 0.01 level. It indicates that there is significant difference in male and female adolescents on social adjustment. Female adolescent's social adjustment is comparatively better than male adolescents. However, emotional adjustment mean value of male adolescents is 14.52 and SD is 7.06 and female adolescents mean value is 15.57 and SD is 6.19. It's 't' value is 2.28. It is significant at 0.05 level. It is interpreted that males are better than females on emotional adjustment. But on overall adjustment there is no significant difference between male and female adolescents. So null hypothesis is partially accepted.

Hypothesis No. 7: There will be no significant difference between urban and rural adolescent on their mothers and fathers acceptance attitude.

Table 4.12: Showing the Mean, SD and 't' Values of Mothers and Fathers Acceptance Attitude of Urban and Rural Adolescents

Family Relationships	Place of Residence	N	Mean	Std. Deviation	Std. Error Mean	t
MA	Urban	419	19.1838	3.71305	.18139	.80
	Rural	428	18.9742	3.92258	.18983	
FA	Urban	419	17.8998	3.65425	.17852	1.31
	Rural	428	17.5761	3.48783	.16879	
PA	Urban	419	37.1384	6.29536	.30755	1.46
	Rural	428	36.4941	6.50293	.31470	

* = 0.05, ** = 0.01 significant level

MA= Mother acceptance, FA = Father acceptance, PA = Parental acceptance

Table 4.12 shows that the mean value of mothers' acceptance attitude of urban adolescents is 19.18 and is 3.71. Similarly rural adolescents mean value is 18.97 and SD is 3.92. The calculated 't' value is 0.80. It is not significant. The mean value of father's acceptance attitude is 17.90 and SD is 3.65.

Similarly rural adolescents mean value is 17.58 and SD is 3.49. It's 't' value is 1.31. It indicates that there is no significant difference between urban and rural adolescent on fathers acceptance attitude. The mean value of parental acceptance attitude of urban adolescents is 37.13 and SD is 6.29. Similarly mean value of rural adolescents is 36.49 and SD is 6.50. The 't' value is 1.46. It indicates that there is no significant difference between urban and rural adolescents on their parental acceptance attitude. It means area of residence is not affecting on parental acceptance attitude.

Hypothesis No. 8: There will be no significant difference between urban and rural adolescents on their mothers and fathers concentration attitude.

Table 4.13: Showing the Mean, SD and 't' Values of Mothers and Fathers Concentration Attitude of Urban and Rural Adolescents

Family Relationships	Place of Residence	N	Mean	Std. Deviation	Std. Error Mean	t
MC	Urban	419	13.7327	3.10273	.15158	1.54
	Rural	428	14.0679	3.20835	.15526	
FC	Urban	419	9.9021	3.04393	.14871	3.26**
	Rural	428	10.6230	3.38399	.16376	
PC	Urban	419	23.6158	5.27999	.25794	2.80**
	Rural	428	24.6534	5.50772	.26654	

* = 0.05, ** = 0.01 significant level

MC = Mothers concentration, FA = Fathers concentration, PA = Parental concentration

Table 4.13 shows that the mean value of mother's concentration attitude of urban adolescents is 13.73 and SD is 3.10, similarly rural adolescents mean is 14.06 and SD is 3.20. It's 't' value is 1.54. It is not significant. It indicates that there is no significant difference between urban and rural adolescents on their mother's concentration attitude. It is interpreted that mothers attitude is not affecting regarding residential area.

With reference to Table 4.13, the mean values of urban and rural adolescents on fathers concentration attitude is 9.90 and 10.62 and SD values are 3.04 and 3.38 respectively. It's 't' value is 3.26. It is significant at 0.01 level. It means fathers of rural areas are more concentrating on their adolescent children than urban fathers.

The urban adolescent's parental concentration attitude mean value is 23.61 and SD is 5.28. Similarly rural adolescents mean value is 24.65 and SD is 5.50. The 't' value is 2.80. It is significant at 0.01 level. Hence, it is interpreted that there is difference between urban and rural adolescents on parental concentration attitude. Rural parents are more concentrating than urban parents to their adolescents children.

Hypothesis No. 9: There will be no significant difference between urban and rural adolescents on their mothers and fathers avoidance attitude.

Table 4.14: Showing the Mean and 't' Value of Mothers and Fathers Avoidance Attitude of Urban and Rural Adolescents

Family Relationships	Place of Residence	N	Mean	Std. Deviation	Std. Error Mean	t
MV	Urban	419	7.9451	6.07011	.29654	7.49**
	Rural	428	11.2576	6.76008	.32714	
FV	Urban	419	7.9737	5.51698	.26952	7.18**
	Rural	428	10.7213	5.60513	.27125	
PV	Urban	419	15.9427	10.92325	.53364	7.74**
	Rural	428	21.9789	11.72882	.56760	

* = 0.05, ** = 0.01 significant level

MC = Mothers Avoidance, FA = Fathers Avoidance, PA = Parental Avoidance

With the reference to above Table 4.14 the mean value and SD value of mothers' avoidance attitude of urban adolescents is 7.95 and 6.07 respectively and means value and SD of rural adolescents is 11.25 and 6.76 respectively. It's calculated 't' value is 7.49. It is significant at 0.01 level. It means that rural mothers are more avoiding their adolescent children than urban mothers.

The mean value and SD of urban adolescents' perception on their father's avoidance attitude is 7.97 and 5.52 respectively, and mean and SD of rural adolescents is 10.62 and 3.38 respectively. It's 't' value is 7.18. It is significant at 0.01 level. There is difference between parental avoidance attitude between urban and rural adolescents.

Regarding parental avoidance attitude the mean and SD value of urban adolescents is 15.94 and 10.92 respectively, and mean and SD of rural adolescents is 21.98 and 11.73 respectively. It's 't' value is 7.74. It is significant at 0.01 level. It is interpreted that there is significant difference between rural and urban adolescents on their perception of parental avoidance attitude. Results show that rural parents are more avoiding their adolescent children than urban parents. So the null hypothesis is rejected.

Hypothesis No. 10: There would be no significant difference between urban and rural adolescents perception on their various dimensions of academic climate.

Table 4.15: The Mean, SD and 't' Value of Various Dimensions on Academic Climate of Urban and Rural Adolescents

Dimensions of Academic Climate	Place of Residence	N	Mean	Std. Deviation	Std. Error Mean	t
PM	Urban	419	26.5298	4.40486	.21519	.03
	Rural	428	26.5199	4.75073	.22990	
IPT	Urban	419	24.4726	3.71871	.18167	1.47
	Rural	428	23.9906	5.59929	.27097	
SP	Urban	419	47.6730	7.64747	.37360	2.21*
	Rural	428	46.3724	9.33892	.45194	
AP	Urban	419	37.1671	5.58156	.27268	4.38**
	Rural	428	35.1686	7.50803	.36334	
ACL Total	Urban	419	139.4773	16.21510	.79216	.60
	Rural	428	138.7635	17.98402	.87031	

* = 0.05, ** = 0.01 significant level

Dimensions of Academic climate PM = Physical Material, IPT = Interpersonal Trust SP = School Provisions, AP = Academic Provisions. ACL TOTAL = overall academic climate

Table 4.15 shows that the mean and SD value of urban and rural adolescent's perception of physical material of their schools. The mean and SD of urban adolescents is 26.53 and 4.40 respectively, and rural adolescents mean and SD is 26.51 and 4.40 respectively. The mean difference is not significant even 0.05 level.

The second dimension of academic climate 'Interpersonal Trust', urban adolescents mean value is 24.47 and SD is 3.71, similarly rural adolescents mean value is 23.99 and SD is 5.59. It is not significant.

Third dimension of academic climate is 'School provisions' urban adolescents mean value is 47.67 and SD value is 7.65. It's 't' value is 2.21. It is significant at 0.05 level.

Forth dimension of academic climate is 'academic provisions'. Urban adolescent's mean value is 37.17 and SD value is 7.50. It's 't' value is 4.38. It is significant at 0.01 level. It means that there is difference between urban and rural adolescent perception on their school provisions and academic provisions. It is interpreted that rural adolescents feel that their schools are not providing school and academic facilities as compared to urban schools. However, on overall academic climate there is no significant difference between urban and rural adolescents perception.

Hypothesis No. 11: There will be no significant difference between urban and rural adolescents on various dimensions of emotional intelligence.

Table 4.16 shows that the mean value of 'inter personal awareness of urban adolescents is 15.42 and SD is 3.51, and rural adolescents mean is 15.10 and SD is 3.64. The 't' value is 1.30. The mean and SD value of intrapersonal awareness of urban adolescents is 14.94 and 3.24 respectively, and rural adolescents mean and SD is 14.75 and 3.18. It's 't' value is 0.86.

Table 4.16: Showing the Mean, SD and 't' Value of Various Dimensions of Emotional Intelligence

Dimensions of EI	Place of Residence	N	Mean	Std. Deviation	Std. Error Mean	t
Intra PA	Urban	419	15.4272	3.51365	.17165	1.30
	Rural	428	15.1054	3.63869	.17609	
Inter PA	Urban	419	14.9499	3.24662	.15861	.86
	Rural	428	14.7541	3.38152	.16364	
Intra PM	Urban	419	17.8353	3.77971	.18465	.09
	Rural	428	17.8595	3.78394	.18312	
Inter PM	Urban	419	16.8138	3.60936	.17633	.40
	Rural	428	16.9110	3.42684	.16584	
EI	Urban	419	65.0263	10.83618	.52938	.54
	Rural	428	64.6300	10.54050	.51009	

* = 0.05, ** = 0.01 significant level

The mean and SD value of Intrapersonal management of urban adolescents is 17.83 and 3.78 respectively. Similarly rural adolescents mean Value is 17.86 and SD value is 3.78.

The dimension of 'interpersonal management', urban adolescents mean is 16.81 and SD value is 3.60. On total emotional intelligence urban adolescents mean 65.02 and SD is 10.84. Similarly rural adolescents mean is 64.63 and SD is 10.54. It's 't' value is 0.54. It is not significant. The hypothesis is accepted. It means that urban and rural adolescents have no significant difference on emotional intelligence.

Hypothesis No. 12: There will be no significant difference between urban and rural adolescents on various areas of adjustment.

Table 4.17 shows that the mean value of home adjustments is 14.38 and SD is 5.08, similarly mean value of rural adolescents is a 15.28 and SD is 4.84. Its 't' value is 2.64. It is significant at 0.01 level.

Table 4.17: Showing the Mean, SD and 't' Value of Various Areas of Adjustment of Male and Female Adolescents

Areas of Adjustment	Place of Residence	N	Mean	Std. Deviation	Std. Error Mean	t
Home	Urban	419	14.3819	5.08608	.24847	2.64**
	Rural	428	15.2834	4.83986	.23422	
Health	Urban	419	10.5632	5.71933	.27941	2.02*
	Rural	428	11.3981	6.26008	.30295	
Social	Urban	419	18.8067	3.55387	.17362	2.26*
	Rural	428	19.4379	4.52149	.21881	
Emotional	Urban	419	14.3341	6.44432	.31483	3.02**
	Rural	428	15.7119	6.79056	.32862	
Overall Adjustment	Urban	419	58.0859	15.82250	.77298	3.36**
	Rural	428	61.8314	16.60645	.80364	

* = 0.05, ** = 0.01 significant level

Regarding health adjustment mean values of urban and rural adolescents are 10.56 and 11.39 respectively. Similarly their SD values are 5.72 and 6.26 respectively. It's 't' value is 2.02. It is significant at 0.05 level.

Mean and SD value of Social adjustment of urban adolescents is 18.80 and 3.55, and rural adolescents mean and SD is 19.43 and 4.52 respectively. It's 't' value is 2.26. It is significant at 0.05 level.

Regarding emotional adjustment mean value of urban adolescents is 14.33 and SD value is 6.44. Similarly mean value of rural adolescents is 15.77 and SD is 6.79. It's 't' value is 3.02. It is significant at 0.01 level.

Table 4.17 shows that overall adjustment mean of urban adolescents is 58.08 and SD is 15.82, whereas mean of rural adolescents is 61.83 and SD is 16.60. The 't' value is 3.36. It is significant at 0.01 level. It means that urban and rural adolescents are difference on home, health social emotional and overall adjustment. So the null hypothesis is rejected. There is difference between urban and rural on home environment, health awareness, social perception and opportunities, way of expression of feelings. The cultural difference can effect on adolescent's adjustment.

Hypothesis No. 13: The various levels of parental acceptance will yield different outcomes of emotional intelligence of adolescents.

Table 4.18: Summary of one-way ANOVA on Emotional Intelligence of Adolescents

Parental Acceptance (IV)

Dimensions of EI		Sum of Squares	df	Mean Square	F	Sig.
Intra PA	Between Groups	182.782	2	91.391	7.248**	.001
	Within Groups	10641.506	845	12.608		
	Total	10824.288	847			
Inter PA	Between Groups	34.871	2	17.436	1.589	.205
	Within Groups	9258.482	845	10.970		
	Total	9293.353	847			
Intra PM	Between Groups	572.688	2	286.344	21.003**	.000
	Within Groups	11506.740	845	13.634		
	Total	12079.429	847			
Inter PM	Between Groups	276.910	2	138.455	11.485**	.000
	Within Groups	10174.476	845	12.055		
	Total	10451.386	847			
Total EI	Between Groups	3378.817	2	1689.408	15.315**	.000
	Within Groups	93100.546	845	110.309		
	Total	96479.362	847			

* = 0.05, ** = 0.01 significant level

Table 4.18 depicted the clear picture of summary of one-way ANOVA where parental acceptance was independent variable while emotional intelligence is a dependent variable. Three groups of adolescents have been made according to different levels of parental acceptance *viz;* high, average and low level of parental acceptance. It is seen from Table 4.18, that these groups are significantly varied on 'intrapersonal awareness'. The 'F' value is significant on 0.01 level (F=7.24, 2.847; P<0.01).

Apart from above findings it is seen that high, average and low parental acceptance groups are not different on 'Interpersonal awareness' (F=1.59, 2,847; P>0.05).

Parental acceptance strongly affects the 'Intrapersonal Management' dimension of emotional intelligence of students. It is noticed that the groups formed in the study are significantly differ on 'Intrapersonal Management' (F=21.00, 2, 847; P<0.01).

The 'F' value 11.48 for 'Interpersonal Management 'is also significant. Hence it is stated that high, average and low level parental acceptance groups are greatly varied.

Finally, so far when one-way ANOVA was performed to find out the group differences on emotional intelligence of adolescents, it is seen that above three groups are yield different outcomes of emotional intelligence. Hence, hypothesis "The various levels of parental acceptance will yield different outcomes of emotional intelligence of adolescents" is strongly rejected in the study.

One way ANOVA gives a global picture and tells that intergroup mean differences are significantly large or not, but it does not tell us weather group 1 *vs* group 2 or group 1 *vs* group 3 comparisons show significantly large mean difference or not. For this purpose statisticians had developed a number of multiple comparison tests. In present study, Tukey's multiple comparison HSD test was employed.

Table 4.19: Mean, SD and Number for Adolescents with High, Average and Low Parental Acceptance on Various Dimensions of Emotional Intelligence (N = 847)

Dimensions of Emotional Intelligence	Parental Acceptance	N	Mean	SD
1	2	3	4	5
Intrapersonal Awareness	High	299	15.6321	3.41902
	Average	392	15.3571	3.42699
	Low	156	14.3205	4.06874
	Total	847	15.2633	3.57696
	High	299	15.0569	3.31664

Condt...

1	2	3	4	5
Interpersonal Awareness	Average	392	14.8367	3.37720
	Low	156	14.4744	3.13245
	Total	847	14.8477	3.31437
Intrapersonal Management	High	299	18.7291	3.38228
	Average	392	17.7526	3.74883
	Low	156	16.3782	4.09775
	Total	847	17.8442	3.77866
Interpersonal Management	High	299	17.5585	3.45912
	Average	392	16.6837	3.48059
	Low	156	15.9872	3.47523
	Total	847	16.8642	3.51481
Total Emotional Intelligence	High	299	66.9431	10.24401
	Average	392	64.6301	10.49776
	Low	156	61.2244	10.99535
	Total	847	64.8194	10.67904

Table 4.20: Tukey's Multiple Comparison HSD Test Showing Group Differences on Emotional Intelligence and it's Various Dimensions

Parental Acceptance (IV)

Dependent Variable	(I) PA Level	(J) PA Level	Mean Difference (I-J)	Std. Error	Sig.	
Intra PA	High PA	Avg PA	.27496	.27264	.57	NS
		Low PA	1.31159(*)	.35070	.001	
	Avg PA	Low PA	1.03663	.33614		NS
Inter PA	High PA	Avg PA	.22012	.25431	.662	NS
		Low PA	.58250	.32712	.177	NS
	Avg PA	Low PA	.36238	.31353	.480	NS
Intra PM	High PA	Avg PA	.97655(*)	.28351	.002	
		Low PA	2.35089(*)	.36468	.000	
	Avg PA	Low PA	1.37435(*)	.34953	.000	
Inter PM	High PA	Avg PA	.87485(*)	.26659	.003	
		Low PA	1.57135(*)	.34292	.000	
	Avg PA	Low PA	.69649	.32868	.087	NS
EI	High PA	Avg PA	2.31304(*)	.80643	.012	
		Low PA	5.71878(*)	1.03732	.000	
	Avg PA	Low PA	3.40574(*)	.99424	.002	

* = 0.05, ** = 0.01 significant level

As stated in above results three groups *viz;* *(i)* high, *(ii)* average and *(iii)* low have been prepared on the basis of score secured by the adolescents on parental acceptance attitude and the effort have been made multiple comparison on emotional intelligence and it's various dimensions. Table 4.20 demonstrates the various values of multiple compressions among groups. The high parental acceptance and average parental groups dose not different on intrapersonal awareness because the mean difference value (I-J = 0 .27) is not significant. However, the significant difference is fond between high and low group of parental acceptance (I- J = 1.31).

It is noticed from Table 4.20 that mean differences for all pairs of parental acceptance are not significant on inter personal awareness.

On the contrary the mean difference for all pairs of parental acceptance is significant on interpersonal management.

Moreover, it is seen that only the mean differences, between high and average as well as high and low parental acceptance (PA) on interpersonal management are significant respectively (I-J=.87 and 1.57).

When multiple comparisons between these groups on emotional intelligence are performed it is seen that all pairs of PA are significant.

Hypothesis No. 14: There exists no significant effect on adjustment of various levels of parental acceptance of adolescents.

It is clear from Table 4.21 that the summary of one way ANOVA where parental acceptance is independent variable while adjustment is a dependent variable. These groups of adolescents have been made according to levels of parental acceptance *viz;* high, average and low level of parental acceptance. It is seen from Table 4.21, that these groups are significantly varied on home adjustment. The 'F' value is significant on 0.01 level (F=7.88, 2,847; P<0.01).

Table 4.21: Shows Summary of one-way ANOVA on Adjustment

Parental Acceptance (IV)

Areas of Adjustment (DV)		Sum of Squares	df	Mean	F	Sig.
Home	Between Groups	384.574	2	192.287	7.882**	.000
	Within Groups	20588.909	845	24.394		
	Total	20973.483	847			
Health	Between Groups	153.504	2	76.752	2.133	.119
	Within Groups	30365.353	845	35.978		
	Total	30518.857	847			
Social	Between Groups	125.300	2	62.650	3.791*	.023
	Within Groups	13948.683	845	16.527		
	Total	14073.983	847			
Emotional	Between Groups	116.895	2	58.448	1.317	.268
	Within Groups	37455.400	845	44.378		
	Total	37572.295	847			
Adjustment	Between Groups	1078.421	2	539.211	2.029	.132
	Within Groups	224304.568	845	265.764		
	Total	225382.989	847			

* = 0.05, ** = 0.01 significant level

Table 4.21 further indicates that high, average and low parental acceptance groups are not different on health adjustment of adolescents (F=2.13, 2,847; P>0.05).

In similar manner, 'F' value of the main effect of parental acceptance (high, average and low) on social adjustment of adolescents come out to be 3.79, which is greater than table value (3.00) at 0.05 level of significance (F = 3.79,2,847; P<0.05).

Apart from above finding it is observed that high, average and low parental acceptance groups are not different on emotional adjustment and overall adjustment. For emotional adjustment 'F' value is 1.31 and overall adjustment 'F' value is 2.02. It is not significant even 0.05 level of significance. So the null hypothesis is partially accepted.

Table 4.22: Mean, SD and Number for Adolescents with High, Average and Low Parental Acceptance on Various Areas of Adjustment (N = 847)

Adjustment Areas	Parental Acceptance	N	Mean	Std. Deviation
Home	High PA	299	14.3579	4.69639
	Avg PA	392	14.6556	5.18667
	Low PA	156	16.2308	4.75034
	Total	847	14.8406	4.97909
Health	High PA	299	10.6522	6.02729
	Avg PA	392	10.8980	5.72559
	Low PA	156	11.8526	6.58523
	Total	847	10.9870	6.00619
Social	High PA	299	19.5652	4.14481
	Avg PA	392	19.0434	3.83758
	Low PA	156	18.4808	4.45113
	Total	847	19.1240	4.07871
Emotional	High PA	299	14.7425	6.88866
	Avg PA	392	14.9770	6.68831
	Low PA	156	15.7949	6.12948
	Total	847	15.0449	6.66421
Total Ajustment	High PA	299	59.3177	16.19313
	Avg PA	392	59.5740	16.49071
	Low PA	156	62.3590	16.03100
	Total	847	59.9965	16.32208

As per Table 4.23 three groups *viz; (i)* high, *(ii)* average and *(iii)* low have been prepared on the basis of scores secured by the adolescents on their perception of parental acceptance attitude and effort has been made for multiple comparison on adjustment its various areas.

Above Table 4.23 stated various values of multiple comparisons among groups. The high parental acceptance and average parental acceptance (PA) does not have difference on home adjustment. Its mean difference value (I-J=0.29), is not significant.

Table 4.23: Tukey's Multiple Compression HSD Test Showing Group Difference on Adjustment and it's Various Areas

(Parental Acceptance IV)

Dependent Variable	(I) PA Level	(J) PA Level	Mean Difference (I-J)	Std. Error	Sig.	95% Confidence Interval	
						Lower Bound	Upper Bound
Home	High PA	Avg PA	-.29775	.37923	.712	-1.1881	.5926
		Low PA	-1.87291(*)	.48781	.000	-3.0182	-.7276
	Avg PA	LowPA	-1.57516(*)	.46755	.002	-2.6729	-.4774
Health	High PA	Avg PA	-.24579	.46055	.855	-1.3271	.8355
		Low PA	-1.20039	.59241	.107	-2.5913	.1905
	AvgPA	Low PA	-.95460	.56781	.213	-2.2877	.3785
Social	High PA	Avg PA	.52185	.31214	.217	-.2110	1.2547
		Low PA	1.08445(*)	.40152	.019	.1417	2.0271
	Avg PA	Low PA	.56260	.38484	.310	-.3409	1.4661
Emotional	High PA	Avg PA	-.23457	.51150	.891	-1.4355	.9664
		Low PA	-1.05240	.65795	.246	-2.5972	.4924
	Avg PA	Low PA	-.81783	.63062	.397	-2.2984	.6628
Ajustment	High PA	Avg PA	-.25625	1.25172	.977	-3.1951	2.6826
		Low PA	-3.04125	1.61011	.143	-6.8215	.7390
	Avg PA	Low PA	-2.78499	1.54324	.169	-6.4083	.8383

* = 0.05, ** = 0.01 significant level

However, the significant mean difference is found between high and low PA groups (I-J=1.87) and average and low parental acceptance group (I-J=1.57).

It is noticed from Table 4.23 that mean differences for all pairs of parental acceptance are not significant on health, emotional and overall adjustment. However the significant mean difference is found between high and low parental acceptance group on social adjustment. (I-J=1.08).

Hypothesis No. 15: There exists no significant effect of levels of parental concentration on emotional intelligence of adolescents.

Table 4.24: Shows Summary of one-way ANOVA on Emotional Intelligence

Parental Concentration (IV)

Dimensions of EI (DV)		Sum of Squares	df	Mean Square	F	Sig.
Intra PA	Between Groups	377.083	2	188.541	15.232**	.000
	Within Groups	10447.205	845	12.378		
	Total	10824.288	847			
Intra PA	Between Groups	265.972	2	132.986	12.433**	.000
	Within Groups	9027.381	845	10.696		
	Total	9293.353	847			
Intra PM	Between Groups	7.409	2	3.705	.259	.772
	Within Groups	12072.019	845	14.303		
	Total	12079.429	847			
Inter PM	Between Groups	82.887	2	41.444	3.374*	.035
	Within Groups	10368.499	845	12.285		
	Total	10451.386	847			
EI	Between Groups	2147.960	2	1073.980	9.609**	.000
	Within Groups	94331.403	845	111.767		
	Total	96479.362	847			

* = 0.05, ** = 0.01 significant level

It is seen from Table 4.24, that three groups of adolescent's perception of their parents' concentration *viz;* high, average and low. Table 4.24 indicates that these groups are significantly different on intrapersonal awareness (F=15.23,2,847; P<0.01), Interpersonal awareness (F=12.43,2, 847; P<0.01), Interpersonal management (F=3.37,2,847; P<0.05) and total emotional intelligence (F=9.60,2, 847; P<0.01).

However, it is noticed that high, average and low groups of parental concentration are not varied on intrapersonal management.

Finally, it is seen that above three groups of parental concentration are yielded different outcomes of emotional intelligence. So hypothesis No. 15 is strongly rejected in the study.

Table 4.25: Mean, SD and Number for Adolescents with High, Average and Low Parental Concentration on Various Dimensions of Emotional Intelligence (N = 847)

Emotional Intelligence Dimensions	Parental Concentration	N	Mean Deviation	Std.
Intrapersonal Awareness	High PC	266	14.4511	3.39025
	Avg PC	385	15.3091	3.56861
	Low PC	196	16.2755	3.58853
	Total	847	15.2633	3.57696
Interpersonal Awareness	High PC	266	14.1466	3.22214
	Avg PC	385	14.9117	3.31702
	Low PC	196	15.6735	3.24322
	Total	847	14.8477	3.31437
Intrapersonal Management	High PC	266	17.7218	3.49415
	Avg PC	385	17.9377	3.80327
	Low PC	196	17.8265	4.10260
	Total	847	17.8442	3.77866
Interpersonal Management	High PC	266	16.5526	3.45415
	Avg PC	385	16.8078	3.48201
	Low PC	196	17.3980	3.61688
	Total	847	16.8642	3.51481
Total Emotional Intelligence	High PC	266	62.8722	9.84592
	Avg PC	385	64.9403	10.57976
	Low PC	196	67.2245	11.47128
	Total	847	64.8194	10.67904

Table 4.26: Shows Tukey's Multiple Compression HSD test Showing Group Differences on Emotional Intelligence and its Various Dimensions

Tukey's HSD

Multiple Compression

Dependent Variable	(I) PC Level	(J) PC Level	Mean Difference (I-J)	Std. Error	Sig.	95% Confidence Interval	
						Lower Bound	Upper Bound
Intra PA	High PC	Avg PC	-.85796(*)	.28051	.006	-1.5166	-.1994
		Low PC	-1.82438(*)	.33119	.000	-2.6020	-1.0468
	Avg PC	Low PC	-.96642(*)	.30872	.005	-1.6912	-.2416
Inter PA	High PC	Avg PC	-.76507(*)	.26075	.010	-1.3773	-.1529
		Low PC	-1.52685(*)	.30787	.000	-2.2497	-.8040
	Avg PC	Low PC	-.76178(*)	.28697	.022	-1.4355	-.0880
Intra PM	High PC	Avg PC	-.21586	.30154	.754	-.9238	.4921
		Low PC	-.10473	.35602	.953	-.9406	.7311
	Avg PC	Low PC	.11113	.33186	.940	-.6680	.8903
Inter PM	High PC	Avg PC	-.25516	.27945	.632	-.9113	.4009
		Low PC	-.84533(*)	.32994	.028	-1.6200	-.0707
	Avg PC	Low PC	-.59017	.30755	.134	-1.3122	.1319
EI	High PC	Avg PC	-2.06808(*)	.84290	.038	-4.0471	-.0891
		Low PC	-4.35231(*)	.99520	.000	-6.6889	-2.0157
	Avg PC	Low PC	-2.28423(*)	.92766	.037	-4.4622	-.1062

* = 0.05, ** = 0.01 significant level

As per above results three groups *viz;* *(i)* high, *(ii)* average and *(iii)* low have been prepared on the basis of scores secured by adolescents on their perception of parental concentration attitude and efforts has been made for multiple comparison on emotional intelligence and its various dimensions.

The significant mean different is found among following groups of parental concentration on intrapersonal awareness group of high and average (I-J= 0 .76) high and low (I-J=1.82) average and low (I-J=0.97).

It is noticed from Table 4.26 that mean differences for all pairs of parental concentration on interpersonal awareness, high and average group (I-J=0.76), high and low (I-J=1.53), average and low (I-J=0.76) significant.

Also mean difference for all pairs of emotional intelligence *e.g.,* high and average (I-J=2.06), high and low (I-J=4.35) and average and low (I-J=2.28) are significant. However, intrapersonal management high and low group difference (I-J=0.85) found significant. For interpersonal management all groups are not significant on parental concentration.

Hypothesis No. 16: There exists no significant effect of various levels of parental concentration on adjustment of adolescents.

Table 4.27 indicates that high, average and low groups of parental concentration perceived by adolescents are significantly differ on home adjustment (F=19.55, 2846; P<0.01).

Table 4.27 further indicates that all groups are significantly differ on health adjustment (F=10.22, 2,847; P<0.01), social adjustment (F=14.99, 2,847; P<0.01), Emotional adjustment (F=22.64 2,847; P<0.01) and overall adjustment (F=30.09, 2, 847; P<0.01). So null hypothesis No. 16 strongly rejected in the study.

Table 4.29 reveals that three groups *viz;* *(i)* high, *(ii)* average and *(iii)* low have been prepared on the basis of scores obtained by adolescents on their perception of parental concentration (PC) and efforts has been made for multiple comparison on adjustment and its various areas.

Table 4.27: Shows Summary of one-way ANOVA on Adjustment

Parental Concentration (IV)

Areas of Adjustment		Sum of Squares	df	Mean Square	F	Sig.
Home	Between Groups	928.422	2	464.211	19.546**	.000
	Within Groups	20045.061	845	23.750		
	Total	20973.483	847			
Health	Between Groups	721.441	2	360.720	10.217**	.000
	Within Groups	29797.417	845	35.305		
	Total	30518.857	847			
Social	Between Groups	482.742	2	241.371	14.989**	.000
	Within Groups	13591.241	845	16.103		
	Total	14073.983	847			
Emotional	Between Groups	1913.408	2	956.704	22.644**	.000
	Within Groups	35658.887	845	42.250		
	Total	37572.295	847			
Ajustment	Between Groups	15002.677	2	7501.339	30.094**	.000
	Within Groups	210380.312	845	249.266		
	Total	225382.989	847			

* = 0.05, ** = 0.01 significant level

Table 4.29 indicates that mean differences for all pairs of PC on adjustment areas found significant. Mean difference between high and average, high and low, average and low groups of parental concentration (I-J=1.63), (I-J=2.80) and (I-J=1.18) respectively on home adjustment.

In the similar manner group differences between high and average (I-J=1.57) and high and low (I-J=2.41) on health adjustment. Group difference between high and average (I-J=1.28), high and low (I-J=1.98) on social adjustment. Group difference between high and average (I-J=2.88) and high and low (I-J=1.98) on social adjustment.

Table 4.28: Mean, SD and Number for Adolescents with High, Average and Low Parental Concentration on Various Areas of Adjustment (N = 847)

Adjustment Areas	Parental Concentration	N	Mean	Std. Deviation
Home	High PC	266	16.2293	4.86691
	Avg PC	385	14.6026	4.95348
	Low PC	196	13.4235	4.72085
	Total	847	14.8406	4.97909
Health	High PC	266	12.2594	6.33144
	Avg PC	385	10.6909	5.89143
	Low PC	196	9.8418	5.47540
	Total	847	10.9870	6.00619
Social	High PC	266	20.1654	4.20993
	Avg PC	385	18.8805	3.91595
	Low PC	196	18.1888	3.92625
	Total	847	19.1240	4.07871
Emotional	High PC	266	17.2143	6.74517
	Avg PC	385	14.3299	6.38584
	Low PC	196	13.5051	6.38227
	Total	847	15.0449	6.66421
Total Ajustment	High PC	266	65.8684	16.01678
	Avg PC	385	58.5039	15.74043
	Low PC	196	54.9592	15.56750
	Total	847	59.9965	16.32208

Group difference between high and average (I-J=2.88) and high and low (I-J=3.71) on emotional adjustment. But overall adjustment group differences among high and average (I-J=7.36), high and low (I-J=10.31) and average and low (I-J=3.54). All groups of parental concentration are significant on overall adjustment.

Hypothesis No. 17: There exists no significant effect of various levels of parental avoidance attitude on emotional intelligence and its four dimensions.

Table 4.29: Tukey's Multiple Comparison HSD test Showing Group Differences on Adjustment and its Various Areas

Dependent Variable	(I) PC Level	(J) PC Level	Mean Difference (I-J)	Std. Error	Sig.	95% Confidence Interval	
						Lower Bound	Upper Bound
Home	High PC	Avg PC	1.62673(*)	.38855	.000	.7145	2.5390
		Low PC	2.80585(*)	.45876	.000	1.7288	3.8830
	Avg PC	Low PC	1.17913(*)	.42762	.016	.1751	2.1831
Health	High PC	Avg PC	1.56849(*)	.47374	.003	.4562	2.6808
		Low PC	2.41756(*)	.55933	.000	1.1043	3.7308
	Avg PC	Low PC	.84907	.52137	.234	-.3750	2.0732
Social	High PC	Avg PC	1.28489(*)	.31995	.000	.5337	2.0361
		Low PC	1.97664(*)	.37776	.000	1.0897	2.8636
	Avg PC	Low PC	.69174	.35212	.122	-.1350	1.5185
Emotinal	High PC	Avg PC	2.88442(*)	.51824	.000	1.6677	4.1012
		Low PC	3.70918(*)	.61188	.000	2.2726	5.1458
	Avg PC	Low PC	.82477	.57035	.318	-.5143	2.1639
Overall Ajustment	High PC	Avg PC	7.36452(*)	1.25878	.000	4.4091	10.3200
		Low PC	10.90924(*)	1.48622	.000	7.4198	14.3987
	Avg PC	Low PC	3.54471(*)	1.38535	.029	.2921	6.7973

* = 0.05, ** = 0.01 significant level

Table 4.30: Shows Summary of the one-way ANOVA on Emotional Intelligence

Parental Avoidance (IV)

Dimensions of EI (DV)		Sum of Squares	df	Mean Square	F	Sig.
Intra PA	Between Groups	942.837	2	471.419	40.265**	.000
	Within Groups	9881.451	845	11.708		
	Total	10824.288	847			
Inter PA	Between Groups	608.397	2	304.198	29.562**	.000
	Within Groups	8684.956	845	10.290		
	Total	9293.353	847			
Intra PM	Between Groups	1018.982	2	509.491	38.878**	.000
	Within Groups	11060.447	845	13.105		
	Total	12079.429	847			
Inter PM	Between Groups	894.878	2	447.439	39.516**	.000
	Within Groups	9556.508	845	11.323		
	Total	10451.386	847			
EI	Between Groups	13582.816	2	6791.408	69.146**	.000
	Within Groups	82896.546	845	98.219		
	Total	96479.362	847			

* = 0.05, ** = 0.01 significant level

Table 4.30 Indicates that three groups of adolescents have been accordingly different levels of parental avoidance attitude, *viz*; high average and low. It is seen that these groups are significantly different on intrapersonal awareness (F=40.27, 2,846; P<0.01), interpersonal awareness (F=29.56, 2, 846; P<0.01) intrapersonal management (F=38.38, 2,846; P<0.01), interpersonal management (F=39.52, 2,846; P<0.01) and total emotional intelligence (F=69.15, 2,846; P<0.01)

It is observed that three groups of parental avoidance attitude are significantly different on emotional intelligence and its four dimensions. So null hypothesis no. 17 is strongly rejected.

Table 4.31: Mean, SD and Number for Adolescents with High, Average and low Parental Avoidance on Various dimensions of Emotional Intelligence (N = 847)

Emotional Intelligence Dimensions	Parental Avoidance	N	Mean	Std. Deviation
Intrapersonal Awareness	High PV	309	14.1553	3.48585
	Avg PV	273	15.1099	3.39263
	Low PV	265	16.7132	3.37561
	Total	847	15.2633	3.57696
Interpersonal Awareness	High PV	309	14.0453	3.22096
	Avg PV	273	14.5788	3.21792
	Low PV	265	16.0604	3.18200
	Total	847	14.8477	3.31437
Intrapersonal Management	High PV	309	16.5663	3.79845
	Avg PV	273	17.9414	3.62947
	Low PV	265	19.2340	3.38977
	Total	847	17.8442	3.77866
Interpersonal Management	High PV	309	15.6958	3.24408
	Avg PV	273	16.8901	3.54939
	Low PV	265	18.2000	3.30770
	Total	847	16.8642	3.51481
Total Emotional Intelligence	High PV	309	60.4628	9.63469
	Avg PV	273	64.5201	10.21427
	Low PV	265	70.2075	9.91012
	Total	847	64.8194	10.67904

In above results three groups *viz; (i)* high, *(ii)* average and *(iii)* low has been made on the basis of scores obtained by the adolescents on their perceived parental avoidance attitude and effort has been made for multiple comparison among these groups, on emotional intelligence and its four dimensions.

Table 4.32 indicates that mean differences in all pairs of parental avoidance attitude on emotional intelligence found significant. Mean difference between high and average group (I-J=.95) high and low (I-J=2.55) and average and low (I-J=1.60) significant on intrapersonal awareness.

Table 4.32: Tukey's Multiple Compression HSD Test Showing Group Differences between Emotional Intelligence and Its Various Dimensions

Tukey's HSD Multiple Compression

Dependent Variable	(I) PV Level	(J) PV Level	Mean Difference (I-J)	Std. Error	Sig.	95% Confidence Interval	
						Lower Bound	Upper Bound
Intra PA	High PV	AVG PV	-.95455(*)	.28421	.002	-1.6218	-.2873
		Low PV	-2.55787(*)	.28648	.000	-3.2305	-1.8853
	Avg PV	Low PV	-1.60332(*)	.29507	.000	-2.2961	-.9105
Inter PA	High PV	Avg PV	-.53345	.26645	.112	-1.1590	.0921
		Low PV	-2.01507(*)	.26858	.000	-2.6456	-1.3845
	Avg PV	Low PV	-1.48162(*)	.27663	.000	-2.1311	-.8321
Intra PM	High PV	Avg PV	-1.37505(*)	.30069	.000	-2.0810	-.6691
		Low PV	-2.66762(*)	.30309	.000	-3.3792	-1.9560
	Avg PV	Low PV	-1.29257(*)	.31218	.000	-2.0255	-.5596
Inter PM	High PV	Avg PV	-1.19432(*)	.27950	.000	-1.8505	-.5381
		Low PV	-2.50421(*)	.28173	.000	-3.1657	-1.8427
	Avg PV	Low PV	-1.30989(*)	.29018	.000	-1.9912	-.6286
EI	High PV	Avg PV	-4.05736(*)	.82319	.000	-5.9901	-2.1246
		Low PV	-9.74476(*)	.82976	.000	-11.6929	-7.7966
	Avg PV	Low PV	-5.68740(*)	.85464	.000	-7.6940	-3.6808

* = 0.05, ** = 0.01 significant level

Group difference between high and low (I-J=2.02) and average and low (I-J=1.48) is significant on interpersonal awareness. The mean difference between high and average (I-J−1.38), high and low (I-J−2.67), average and low (I-J−1.29) is significant on intrapersonal management.

Group high and average (I-J=1.19), high and low (I-J=2.50), average and low (I-J=1.31) is significant on interpersonal management.

Group high and average (I-J=4.06), high and low (I-J=9.74) and average and low (I-J=5.69) is significant on emotional intelligence.

Hypothesis No. 18: There exists no significant effect of various levels of parental avoidance on adjustment and its four areas.

Table 4.33: Shows Summary of one-way ANOVA on Adjustment

Parental Avoidance (IV)

Areas of Adjustment (DV)		Sum of Squares	df	Mean Square	F	Sig.
Home	Between Groups	3502.221	2	1751.111	84.592**	.000
	Within Groups	17471.262	845	20.701		
	Total	20973.483	847			
Health	Between Groups	3190.969	2	1595.485	49.275**	.000
	Within Groups	27327.888	845	32.379		
	Total	30518.857	847			
Social	Between Groups	532.342	2	266.171	16.589**	.000
	Within Groups	13541.642	845	16.045		
	Total	14073.983	847			
Emotional	Between Groups	3292.961	2	1646.481	40.538**	.000
	Within Groups	34279.334	845	40.615		
	Total	37572.295	847			
Adjustment	Between Groups	37847.390	2	18923.695	85.166**	.000
	Within Groups	187535.600	845	222.199		
	Total	225382.989	847			

* = 0.05, ** = 0.01 significant level

Table 4.33 indicates that high, average and low groups of parental avoidance perceived by adolescents are significantly differ on home adjustment (F=84.59,2,847; P<0.01), health adjustment (F=49.28,2,847; P<0.01), social adjustment (F=16.59,2,847; P<0.01) emotional adjustment (F=40.54 , 2,847; P<0.01) and over all adjustment (F=85.16 , 2,847; P<0.01) So the null hypothesis No. 18 is strongly rejected.

Table 4.34: Mean, SD and Number for Adolescents with High, Average and Low Parental Avoidance on Various Areas of Adjustment (N = 847)

Adjustment Areas	Parental Avoidance	N	Mean	SD
Home	High PV	309	17.1845	4.97412
	Avg PV	273	14.7179	4.34508
	Low PV	265	12.2340	4.22631
	Total	847	14.8406	4.97909
Health	High PV	309	13.1748	6.65391
	Avg PV	273	10.9780	5.36939
	Low PV	265	8.4453	4.70713
	Total	847	10.9870	6.00619
Social	High PV	309	20.1294	4.07113
	Avg PV	273	18.8168	4.17487
	Low PV	265	18.2679	3.74165
	Total	847	19.1240	4.07871
Emotional	High PV	309	17.0259	6.44704
	Avg PV	273	15.4872	6.26035
	Low PV	265	12.2792	6.40115
	Total	847	15.0449	6.66421
Total Ajustment	High PV	309	67.5146	16.12625
	Avg PV	273	60.0000	14.20957
	Low PV	265	51.2264	14.10437
	Total	847	59.9965	16.32208

Table 4.35: Shows Tukey's Multiple Comparison HSD Test Showing Group Differences on Adjustment and its Four Areas

Dependent Variable	(I) PV Level	(J) PV Level	Mean Difference (I-J)	Std. Error	Sig.	95% Confidence Interval	
						Lower Bound	Upper Bound
Home	High PV	Avg PV	2.46652(*)	.37791	.000	1.5792	3.3538
		Low PV	4.95050(*)	.38093	.000	4.0561	5.8449
	Avg PV	Low PV	2.48399(*)	.39235	.000	1.5628	3.4052
Health	High PV	Avg PV	2.19674(*)	.47264	.000	1.0870	3.3064
		Low PV	4.72947(*)	.47642	.000	3.6109	5.8480
	Avg PV	Low PV	2.53274(*)	.49070	.000	1.3806	3.6848
Social	High PV	Avg PV	1.31260(*)	.33271	.000	.5314	2.0938
		Low PV	1.86153(*)	.33537	.000	1.0741	2.6489
	Avg PV	Low PV	.54893	.34542	.251	-.2621	1.3599
Emotional	High PV	Avg PV	1.53871(*)	.52935	.010	.2959	2.7816
		Low PV	4.74664(*)	.53358	.000	3.4939	5.9994
	Avg PV	Low PV	3.20793(*)	.54958	.000	1.9176	4.4983
Ajustment	High PV	Avg PV	7.51456(*)	1.23815	.000	4.6076	10.4215
		Low PV	16.28815(*)	1.24803	.000	13.3580	19.2183
	Avg PV	Low PV	8.77358(*)	1.28546	.000	5.7555	11.7916

* = 0.05, ** = 0.01 significant level

Table 4.35 indicates that mean differences for all pairs of parental avoidance on adjustment found significant. Group high and average (I-J=2.47) high and low (I-J=4.95) average and low (I-J=2.48) on home adjustment, group high and average (I-J=2.19) high and low (I-J=4.73) and average and low (I-J=2.53) on health adjustment. Group high and average (I-J=1.31), high and low (I-J=1.86) on social adjustment, group high and average (I-J=1.54), high and low (I-J=4.75), average and low (I-J=3.21) on emotional adjustment. And group high and average (I-J=7.51) high and low (I-J=16.29), average and low (I-J=8.77) on overall adjustment.

Hypothesis No. 19: There exists no significant effect of various levels of physical material (a dimension of academic climate) on emotional intelligence.

Table 4.36: Shows Summary of one-way ANOVA on Emotional Intelligence

Physical Material (a dimension of academic climate) (IV)

Dimensions of EI (DV)		Sum of Squares	df	Mean Squares	F	Sig.
Intra PA	Between Groups	318.734	2	159.367	12.803**	.000
	Within Groups	10505.554	845	12.447		
	Total	10824.288	847			
Inter PA	Between Groups	400.525	2	200.263	19.007**	.000
	Within Groups	8892.828	845	10.537		
	Total	9293.353	847			
Intra PM	Between Groups	401.057	2	200.528	14.492**	.000
	Within Groups	11678.372	845	13.837		
	Total	12079.429	847			
Inter PM	Between Groups	560.603	2	280.302	23.919**	.000
	Within Groups	9890.783	845	11.719		
	Total	10451.386	847			
EI	Between Groups	6604.883	2	3302.441	31.013**	.000
	Within Groups	89874.480	845	106.486		
	Total	96479.362	847			

* = 0.05, ** = 0.01 significant level

Table 4.36 indicates that high, average and low levels of physical material (a dimension of academic climate) perceived by the adolescents are significantly differ on emotional intelligence and its four factors. It is seen that these groups are significantly different on intrapersonal awareness (F=12.80,2,847; P<0.01), interpersonal awareness (F=19.00,2, 847; P<0.01), intrapersonal management (F=14.49, 2,847; P<0.01), interpersonal management (F=23.92, 2,847; P<0.01) and emotional intelligence (F=31.01,2,847; P<0.01).

It is seen that three groups of physical material of academic climate are significantly different on emotional intelligence and its four dimensions. So null hypothesis No. 19 is strongly rejected.

Table 4.37: Mean, SD and Number for Adolescents with High, Average and low Physical Material on Various Dimensions of Emotional Intelligence (N = 847)

EI Dimensions	Physical Material	N	Mean Deviation	Std.
Intrapersonal Awareness	High PM	496	15.7601	3.51690
	Avg PM	198	14.7879	3.39385
	Low PM	153	14.2680	3.72934
	Total	847	15.2633	3.57696
Interpersonal Awareness	High PM	496	15.4234	3.14790
	Avg PM	198	14.1263	3.28034
	Low PM	153	13.9150	3.50554
	Total	847	14.8477	3.31437
Intrapersonal Management	High PM	496	18.3911	3.68840
	Avg PM	198	17.3788	3.57273
	Low PM	153	16.6732	3.99808
	Total	847	17.8442	3.77866
Interpersonal Management	High PM	496	17.5323	3.54808
	Avg PM	198	16.1616	3.29191
	Low PM	153	15.6078	3.16692
	Total	847	16.8642	3.51481
Total Emotional Intelligence	High PM	496	67.1069	10.36850
	Avg PM	198	62.4545	10.44616
	Low PM	153	60.4641	9.98751
	Total	847	64.8194	10.67904

In above Table 4.38 depict that three groups (*e.g.*, *(i)* high, *(ii)* average and *(iii)* low) has been made on the basis of scores

Table 4.38: Shows Tukey's Multiple Comparison HSD Test Showing Group Differences on Emotional Intelligence and Its Four Dimensions

Tukey's HSD — Multiple Comparison

Dependent Variable	(I) PM Level	(J) PM Level	Mean Difference (I-J)	Std. Error	Sig.	95% Confidence Interval	
						Lower Bound	Upper Bound
Intra PA	High PM	Avg PM	.97220(*)	.29658	.003	.2759	1.6685
		Low PM	1.49211(*)	.32627	.000	.7261	2.2581
	Avg PM	Low PM	.51990	.37976	.358	-.3717	1.4115
Inter PA	High PM	Avg PM	1.29712(*)	.27287	.000	.6565	1.9378
		Low PM	1.50835(*)	.30018	.000	.8036	2.2131
	Avg PM	Low PM	.21123	.34940	.818	-.6091	1.0316
Intra PM	High PM	Avg PM	1.01234(*)	.31270	.004	.2782	1.7465
		Low PM	1.71793(*)	.34400	.000	.9103	2.5256
	Avg PM	Low PM	.70559	.40040	.183	-.2345	1.6457
Inter PM	High PM	Avg PM	1.37064(*)	.28777	.000	.6950	2.0463
		Low PM	1.92441(*)	.31658	.000	1.1811	2.6677
	Avg PM	Low PM	.55377	.36848	.290	-.3114	1.4189
EI	High PM	Avg PM	4.65231(*)	.86747	.000	2.6156	6.6890
		Low PM	6.64280(*)	.95430	.000	4.4023	8.8833
	Avg PM	Low PM	1.99049	1.11077	.173	-.6174	4.5984

* = 0.05, ** = 0.01 significant level

obtained by the adolescents on their perception about academic climate and efforts has been made for multiple comparison among these three groups on emotional intelligence and its dimensions.

Table 4.38 indicates that mean differences of following pairs found significant. On intrapersonal awareness high and average group (I-J=0.97), and high and low group (I-J=1.49) difference is significant. On interpersonal awareness high and average (I-J=1.29) and high and low (I-J=1.51) group difference is significant.

On intrapersonal management high and average (I-J=1.01) and high and low (I-J=1.72) group mean difference is significant. For interpersonal management high and average group (I-J=1.37) and high and low group (I-J=1.92) mean difference is significant. For overall emotional intelligence high and average (I-J=4.65) and high and low (I-J=6.64) group mean difference is significant.

Hypothesis No. 20: There exists no significant effect of various levels of physical material (a dimension of academic climate) on adjustment.

Table 4.39: Shows Summary of one-way ANOVA on Adjustment
Physical material (a dimension of academic climate) (IV)

Areas of Adjustment (DV)		Sum of Squares	df	Mean Squares	F	Sig.
Home	Between Groups	1242.067	2	621.034	26.564**	.000
	Within Groups	19731.416	845	23.378		
	Total	20973.483	847			
Health	Between Groups	1099.945	2	549.972	15.778**	.000
	Within Groups	29418.913	845	34.857		
	Total	30518.857	847			
Social	Between Groups	18.716	2	9.358	.562	.570
	Within Groups	14055.267	845	16.653		
	Total	14073.983	847			
Emotional	Between Groups	573.104	2	286.552	6.537**	.002
	Within Groups	36999.191	845	43.838		
	Total	37572.295	847			
Overall Ajustment	Between Groups	9090.015	2	4545.008	17.735**	.000
	Within Groups	216292.974	845	256.271		
	Total	225382.989	847			

* = 0.05, ** = 0.01 significant level

Table 4.39 indicates that high, average and low levels of physical material (a dimension of academic climate) perceived by the adolescents on significantly differ on adjustment and its some areas. It is seen that three groups are significantly different on home adjustment (F=26.56, 2,847; P<0.01), health (F=15.79,2,847; P<0.01) and over all adjustment (F=17.73, 2,847; P<0.01). However these groups are not different on social adjustment. Null hypothesis is partially rejected.

Table 4.40: Mean, SD and Number for Adolescents with High, Average and low Physical Material on Various Areas of Adjustment (N = 847)

Adjustment Areas	Physical Material	N	Mean Deviation	Std.
Home	High PM	496	13.8246	4.73366
	Avg PM	198	16.1566	4.95879
	Low PM	153	16.4314	4.99706
	Total	847	14.8406	4.97909
Health	High PM	496	10.0544	5.51317
	Avg PM	198	11.9444	6.13734
	Low PM	153	12.7712	6.76339
	Total	847	10.9870	6.00619
Social	High PM	496	19.0202	3.91263
	Avg PM	198	19.3838	4.27650
	Low PM	153	19.1242	4.34881
	Total	847	19.1240	4.07871
Emotional	High PM	496	14.3629	6.85679
	Avg PM	198	15.8182	6.43178
	Low PM	153	16.2549	6.05732
	Total	847	15.0449	6.66421
Total Ajustment	High PM	496	57.2621	15.77531
	Avg PM	198	63.3030	16.21897
	Low PM	153	64.5817	16.48070
	Total	847	59.9965	16.32208

Table 4.41: Shows Tukey's Multiple Comparison HSD Test Showing Groups Difference on Adjustment

Dependent Variable	(I) PM Level	(J) PM Level	Mean Difference (I-J)	Std. Error	Sig.	95% Confidence Interval	
						Lower Bound	Upper Bound
Home	High PM	Avg PM	-2.33197(*)	.40646	.000	-3.2863	-1.3777
		Low PM	-2.60678(*)	.44714	.000	-3.6566	-1.5570
	Avg PM	Low PM	-.27481	.52045	.858	-1.4968	.9471
Health	High PM	Avg PM	-1.89001(*)	.49630	.000	-3.0553	-.7248
		Low PM	-2.71681(*)	.54598	.000	-3.9987	-1.4349
	Avg PM	Low PM	-.82680	.63550	.395	-2.3189	.6653
Social	High PM	Avg PM	-.36368	.34305	.539	-1.1691	.4417
		Low PM	-.10402	.37738	.959	-.9901	.7820
	Avg PM	Low PM	.25966	.43926	.825	-.7717	1.2910
Emotional	High PM	Avg PM	-1.45528(*)	.55658	.025	-2.7621	-.1485
		Low PM	-1.89200(*)	.61229	.006	-3.3296	-.4544
	Avg PM	Low PM	-.43672	.71269	.813	-2.1100	1.2366
Overall Ajustment	High PM	Avg PM	-6.04093(*)	1.34572	.000	-9.2005	-2.8814
		Low PM	-7.31960(*)	1.48042	.000	-10.7954	-3.8438
	Avg PM	Low PM	-1.27867	1.72316	.739	-5.3244	2.7670

* = 0.05, ** = 0.01 significant level

Table 4.41 indicates that mean difference of following pairs found significant. On home adjustment high and average group (I-J=2.33), high and low (I-J=2.61), on health adjustment high and average group (I-J=1.89) high and low (I-J=2.72), on emotional adjustment high and average group (I-J=1.45), high and low group (I-J=1.89) on over all adjustment high and average group (I-J=6.04) high and low (I-J=7.32). However no any significant difference found in the groups on social adjustment.

Hypothesis No. 21: There exists no significant effect of various levels of Inter personal Trust (a dimension of academic climate) on emotional intelligence.

Table 4.42: Shows Summary of the one-way ANOVA on Emotional Intelligence

Interpersonal Trust (a dimension of academic climate) (IV)

Dimensions of EI (DV)		Sum of Squares	df	Mean Squares	F	Sig.
Intra PA	Between Groups	347.016	2	173.508	13.977**	.000
	Within Groups	10477.272	845	12.414		
	Total	10824.288	847			
Inter PA	Between Groups	199.571	2	99.785	9.261**	.000
	Within Groups	9093.782	845	10.775		
	Total	9293.353	847			
Intra PM	Between Groups	645.877	2	322.938	23.839**	.000
	Within Groups	11433.552	845	13.547		
	Total	12079.429	847			
Inter PM	Between Groups	337.388	2	168.694	14.077**	.000
	Within Groups	10113.998	845	11.983		
	Total	10451.386	847			
EI	Between Groups	5736.832	2	2868.416	26.679**	.000
	Within Groups	90742.531	845	107.515		
	Total	96479.362	847			

* = 0.05, ** = 0.01 significant level

Table 4.42 shows that high, average and low levels of interpersonal trust (a dimension of academic climate) perceived by the adolescents are significantly differ on emotional intelligence and its four dimensions. These groups are significantly different on Intrapersonal awareness (F=13.98,2,847; P<0.01), Interpersonal awareness (F=12.41,2, 847; P<0.01), Interpersonal management (F=23.84,2,847; P<0.01) and overall Emotional intelligence (F=26.68,2,847; P<0.01). It is observed that three groups of interpersonal trust are significantly different on emotional intelligence and its four dimensions. So null hypothesis No. 21 is rejected.

Table 4.43: Mean, SD and Number for Adolescents with High, Average and low Interpersonal Trust on Various Dimensions of Emotional Intelligence (N = 847)

EI Dimensions	Interpersonal Trust	N	Mean	SD
Intrapersonal Awareness	High IPT	567	15.6437	3.49559
	Avg IPT	130	15.1308	3.60531
	Low IPT	150	13.9400	3.55632
	Total	847	15.2633	3.57696
Interpersonal Awareness	High IPT	567	15.1235	3.34351
	Avg IPT	130	14.8231	3.29309
	Low IPT	150	13.8267	3.02949
	Total	847	14.8477	3.31437
Intrapersonal Management	High IPT	567	18.4392	3.60351
	Avg IPT	130	17.0385	3.86879
	Low IPT	150	16.2933	3.80135
	Total	847	17.8442	3.77866
Interpersonal Management	High IPT	567	17.2981	3.35124
	Avg IPT	130	16.2308	3.92278
	Low IPT	150	15.7733	3.44885
	Total	847	16.8642	3.51481
Total Emotional Intelligence	High IPT	567	66.5220	10.47186
	Avg IPT	130	63.1462	10.15241
	Low IPT	150	59.8333	10.15941
	Total	847	64.8194	10.67904

Table 4.44: Shows Tukey's Multiple Comparison HSD Test Showing Group Differences on Emotional Intelligence and Its Four Dimensions

Dependent Variable	(I) IPA Level	(J) IPA Level	Mean Difference (I-J)	Std. Error	Sig.	95% Confidence Interval	
						Lower Bound	Upper Bound
Intra PA	High IPT	Avg IPT	.51297	.34261	.293	-.2914	1.3174
		Low IPT	1.70374(*)	.32350	.000	.9442	2.4633
	Avg IPT	Low IPT	1.19077(*)	.42220	.014	.1995	2.1820
Inter PA	High IPT	Avg IPT	.30038	.31919	.614	-.4490	1.0498
		Low IPT	1.29679(*)	.30139	.000	.5892	2.0044
	Avg IPT	Low IPT	.99641(*)	.39334	.031	.0729	1.9199
Intra PM	High IPT	Avg IPT	1.40069(*)	.35791	.000	.5604	2.2410
		Low IPT	2.14582(*)	.33794	.000	1.3524	2.9393
	Avg IPT	Low IPT	.74513	.44104	.210	-.2904	1.7806
Inter PM	High IPT	Avg IPT	1.06729(*)	.33662	.004	.2770	1.8576
		Low IPT	1.52473(*)	.31784	.000	.7785	2.2710
	Avg IPT	Low IPT	.45744	.41481	.513	-.5165	1.4314
EI	High IPT	Avg IPT	3.37589(*)	1.00829	.002	1.0086	5.7432
		Low IPT	6.68871(*)	.95204	.000	4.4535	8.9240
	AVG IPT	Low IPT	3.31282(*)	1.24250	.021	.3956	6.2300

* = 0.05, ** = 0.01 significant level

Table 4.44 indicated that three groups (*e.g.*, *(i)* high, *(ii)* average and *(iii)* low) has been made on the basis of scores obtained by the adolescents on their perception about academic climate and effort has been made for multiple comparison among these groups on emotional intelligence.

Table 4.44 shows the mean differences of following pairs found significant. On intrapersonal awareness high and low group (I-J=1.70) average and low group (I-J=1.19), on interpersonal awareness high and low group (I-J=1.29), average and low (I-J=0.99) on interpersonal management high and average group (I-J=1.40), high and low (I-J=2.15), on interpersonal management, high and average (I-J=1.06), high and low (I-J = 1.52), on emotional intelligence, high and average (I-J 3.36), high and low (I-J=6.68), average and low (I-J=3.31).

Hypothesis No. 22: There exists no significant effect of various levels of Inter personal Trust (a dimension of academic climate) on adjustment.

Table 4.45: Shows Summary of one-way ANOVA on Adjustment

Interpersonal Trust (a dimension of academic climate) (IV)

Areas of Adjustment (DV)		Sum of Squares	df	Mean Squares	F	Sig.
Home	Between Groups	638.187	2	319.093	13.244**	.000
	Within Groups	20335.296	845	24.094		
	Total	20973.483	847			
Health	Between Groups	1623.775	2	811.888	23.715**	.000
	Within Groups	28895.082	845	34.236		
	Total	30518.857	847			
Social	Between Groups	21.569	2	10.785	.648	.523
	Within Groups	14052.414	845	16.650		
	Total	14073.983	847			
Emotional	Between Groups	683.764	2	341.882	7.822**	.000
	Within Groups	36888.531	845	43.707		
	Total	37572.295	847			
Ajustment	Between Groups	8631.514	2	4315.757	16.805**	.000
	Within Groups	216751.475	845	256.815		
	Total	225382.989	847			

* = 0.05, ** = 0.01 significant level

Table 4.45 indicates that, high average and low levels of Inter personal Trust (a dimension of academic climate) perceived by the adolescents are significantly differ on adjustment and its some areas.

It is observed that three groups are significantly different on home adjustment (F=13.24, 2,847; P<0.01), health (F=23.72, 2,847; P<0.01), emotional (F=7.82, 2,847; P<0.01.) and overall adjustment (F=16.80, 2,847; P<0.01.). However these groups are not differ on social adjustment. So hypothesis No. 22 is partially rejected.

Table 4.46: Mean, SD and Number for Adolescents with High, Average and low Interpersonal Trust on Various Areas of Adjustment (N = 847)

Adjustment Areas	Interpersonal Trust	N	Mean	SD
Home	High IPT	567	14.2310	4.97817
	Avg IPT	130	16.0154	5.16395
	Low IPT	150	16.1267	4.38774
	Total	847	14.8406	4.97909
Health	High IPT	567	10.1199	5.64714
	Avg IPT	130	11.5692	6.14166
	Low IPT	150	13.7600	6.33482
	Total	847	10.9870	6.00619
Social	High IPT	567	19.0300	4.13818
	Avg IPT	130	19.4769	3.97124
	Low IPT	150	19.1733	3.95061
	Total	847	19.1240	4.07871
Emotional	High IPT	567	14.4780	7.01481
	Avg IPT	130	15.4538	6.32469
	Low IPT	150	16.8333	5.10088
	Total	847	15.0449	6.66421
Total Ajustment	High IPT	567	57.8589	16.48968
	Avg IPT	130	62.5154	16.25057
	Low IPT	150	65.8933	13.89904
	Total	847	59.9965	16.32208

Table 4.47: Shows Tukey's Multiple Comparison HSD Test Showing Group Differences on Adjustment

Dependent Variable	(I) IPA Level	(J) IPA Level	Mean Difference (I-J)	Std. Error	Sig.	95% Confidence Interval	
						Lower Bound	Upper Bound
Home	High IPT	Avg IPT	-1.78434(*)	.47732	.001	-2.9050	-.6637
		Low IPT	-1.89563(*)	.45069	.000	-2.9538	-.8375
	Avg IPT	Low IPT	-.11128	.58819	.980	-1.4923	1.2697
Health	High IPT	Avg IPT	-1.44930(*)	.56898	.030	-2.7852	-.1134
		Low IPT	-3.64007(*)	.53723	.000	-4.9014	-2.3787
	Avg IPT	Low IPT	-2.19077(*)	.70114	.005	-3.8369	-.5446
Social	High IPT	Avg IPT	-.44694	.39679	.498	-1.3785	.4847
		Low IPT	-.14335	.37465	.922	-1.0230	.7363
	Avg IPT	Low IPT	.30359	.48895	.809	-.8444	1.4516
Emotinal	High IPT	Avg IPT	-.97589	.64288	.283	-2.4853	.5335
		Low IPT	-2.35538(*)	.60701	.000	-3.7806	-.9302
	Avg IPT	Low IPT	-1.37949	.79220	.190	-3.2395	.4805
Ajustment	High IPT	Avg IPT	-4.65648(*)	1.55834	.008	-8.3152	-.9977
		Low IPT	-8.03443(*)	1.47140	.000	-11.4891	-4.5798
	AVG IPT	Low IPT	-3.37795	1.92031	.184	-7.8866	1.1307

* = 0.05, ** = 0.01 significant level

As per Table 4.47 three groups (*e.g.*, *(i)* high, *(ii)* average and *(iii)* low) has been made on the basis of scores by the adolescents on their perception about Interpersonal Trust (IPT) (a dimension of academic climate) and efforts has been made for multiple compression among these three groups on adjustment and its four areas.

As per above result, mean difference of following pairs found significant. On home adjustment, high and average group (I-J=1.78), high and low (I-J=1.89), on health ,high and average group (I-J=1.45), high and low (I-J=3.64), average and low (I-J=2.19), on emotional, high and low group (I-J=2.35), over all adjustment, high and average group (I-J=4.66) and high and low (I-J=8.03). However, there is no any significant difference on social adjustment.

Hypothesis No. 23: There exists no significant effect of various levels of School Provisions (a dimension of academic climate) on emotional intelligence.

Table 4.48: Shows Summary of one-way ANOVA on Emotional Intelligence

School Provisions (a dimension of academic climate) (IV)

Dimensions of EI (DV)		Sum of Squares	df	Mean Squares	F	Sig.
Intra PA	Between Groups	459.998	2	229.999	18.730**	.000
	Within Groups	10364.290	845	12.280		
	Total	10824.288	847			
Inter PA	Between Groups	394.096	2	197.048	18.688**	.000
	Within Groups	8899.257	845	10.544		
	Total	9293.353	847			
Intra PM	Between Groups	739.710	2	369.855	27.528**	.000
	Within Groups	11339.718	845	13.436		
	Total	12079.429	847			
Inter PM	Between Groups	394.638	2	197.319	16.560**	.000
	Within Groups	10056.748	845	11.916		
	Total	10451.386	847			
EI	Between Groups	7685.730	2	3842.865	36.527**	.000
	Within Groups	88793.633	845	105.206		
	Total	96479.362	847			

* = 0.05, ** = 0.01 significant level

Table 4.48 shows that high, average and low levels of school provisions (a dimension of academic climate) perceived by the adolescents are significantly differ on emotional intelligence and its four dimension. These groups are significantly different on Intrapersonal awareness (F=18.73, 2,847; P<0.01), interpersonal awareness (F=18.69, 2,847; P<0.01). Intrapersonal management (F=27.52,2,847; P<0.01), interpersonal management (F=16.56,2,847; P<0.01) and total emotional intelligence (F=36.53,2,847; P<0.01).

It is found that three groups of school provisions are significantly different on emotional intelligence and its four dimensions. So null hypothesis No. 23 is strongly rejected.

Table 4.49: Mean, SD and Number for Adolescents with High, Average and low School Provision on Various Dimensions of Emotional Intelligence (N = 847)

EI Dimensions	School Provision	N	Mean	SD
Intrapersonal Awareness	High SP	397	15.8086	3.45806
	Avg SP	200	15.5950	3.36714
	Low SP	250	14.1320	3.68032
	Total	847	15.2633	3.57696
Interpersonal Awareness	High SP	397	15.4332	3.22533
	Avg SP	200	14.9500	3.19036
	Low SP	250	13.8360	3.32586
	Total	847	14.8477	3.31437
Intrapersonal Management	High SP	397	18.5919	3.62994
	Avg SP	200	18.1300	3.74073
	Low SP	250	16.4280	3.66093
	Total	847	17.8442	3.77866
Interpersonal Management	High SP	397	17.2645	3.44848
	Avg SP	200	17.3850	3.56656
	Low SP	250	15.8120	3.36302
	Total	847	16.8642	3.51481
Total Emotional Intelligence	High SP	397	67.0982	10.14082
	Avg SP	200	66.0600	10.54668
	Low SP	250	60.2080	10.20575
	Total	847	64.8194	10.67904

Table 4.50: Shows Tukey's Multiple Compression HSD Test Showing Group Differences on Emotional Intelligence and it's Four Dimensions

Dependent Variable	(I) SP Level	(J) SP Level	Mean Difference (I-J)	Std. Error	Sig.	95% Confidence Interval	
						Lower Bound	Upper Bound
Intra PA	High SP	Avg SP	.21356	.30386	.762	-.4999	.9270
		Low SP	1.67656(*)	.28293	.000	1.0123	2.3409
	Avg SP	LOW SP	1.46300(*)	.33245	.000	.6825	2.2435
Inter PA	High SP	Avg SP	.48325	.28157	.200	-.1778	1.1443
		Low SP	1.59725(*)	.26218	.000	.9817	2.2128
	Avg SP	Low SP	1.11400(*)	.30805	.001	.3907	1.8373
Intra PM	High SP	Avg SP	.46194	.31784	.314	-.2843	1.2082
		Low SP	2.16394(*)	.29595	.000	1.4691	2.8588
	Avg SP	Low SP	1.70200(*)	.34774	.000	.8856	2.5184
Inter PM	High SP	Avg SP	-.12052	.29932	.915	-.8233	.5822
		Low SP	1.45248(*)	.27870	.000	.7981	2.1068
	Avg SP	Low SP	1.57300(*)	.32748	.000	.8041	2.3419
EI	High SP	Avg SP	1.03824	.88940	.473	-1.0499	3.1264
		Low SP	6.89024(*)	.82815	.000	4.9459	8.8346
	Avg SP	Low SP	5.85200(*)	.97306	.000	3.5674	8.1366

* = 0.05, ** = 0.01 significant level

Table 4.50 indicates that three groups (*e.g., (i)* high, *(ii)* average and *(iii)* low) has been made on the basis of scores obtained by the adolescents on their perception about academic climate (school provisions) and efforts has been made for multiple compression among these groups on emotional intelligence.

Table 4.50 shows that the mean differences of following pairs found significant on intrapersonal awareness, high and low group (I-J=1.68), average and low group (I-J=1.46), on interpersonal awareness high and low group (I-J=1.59), average and low group (I-J=1.11), on intrapersonal management, high and low (I-J=2.16), average and low group (I-J=2.70), on interpersonal management, high and low group (I-J=1.45), average and low group (I-J=1.57) and on overall EI group, high and low group (I-J=6.89), and average and low group (I-J=5.85).

Hypothesis No. 24: There exists no significant effect of various levels of school provisions (a dimension of academic climate) on adjustment.

Table 4.51: Shows Summary of one-way ANOVA on Adjustment

School Provisions (a dimension of academic climate) (IV)

Areas of Adjustment (DV)		Sum of Squares	df	Mean Squares	F	Sig.
Home	Between Groups	1337.333	2	668.667	28.741**	.000
	Within Groups	19636.149	845	23.266		
	Total	20973.483	847			
Health	Between Groups	1487.563	2	743.782	21.623**	.000
	Within Groups	29031.294	845	34.397		
	Total	30518.857	847			
Social	Between Groups	100.976	2	50.488	3.050*	.048
	Within Groups	13973.007	845	16.556		
	Total	14073.983	847			
Emotional	Between Groups	1693.914	2	846.957	19.924**	.000
	Within Groups	35878.381	845	42.510		
	Total	37572.295	847			
Ajustment	Between Groups	15670.417	2	7835.209	31.533**	.000
	Within Groups	209712.572	845	248.475		
	Total	225382.989	847			

* = 0.05, ** = 0.01 significant level

Table 4.51 indicates that high, average and low level of school provisions (a dimension of academic climate) perceived by the adolescents are significantly differ on adjustment and its four areas. It is seen that three groups are significantly different on home adjustment (F=28.74,2,847; P<0.01) Health adjustment (F=21.62,2,847; P<0.01), social adjustment (F=19.92,2,847; P<0.01), and over all adjustment (F=31.53,2,847; P<0.01). So null hypothesis is strongly rejected.

Table 4.52: Mean, SD and Number for Adolescents with High, Average and Low School Provisions on Various Areas of Adjustment (N = 847)

Adjustment Areas	School Provision	N	Mean	SD
Home	High SP	397	13.6020	4.90905
	Avg SP	200	15.2050	4.54713
	Low SP	250	16.5160	4.89998
	Total	847	14.8406	4.97909
Health	High SP	397	9.7632	5.57088
	Avg SP	200	11.0550	5.38675
	Low SP	250	12.8760	6.63663
	Total	847	10.9870	6.00619
Social	High SP	397	18.8791	4.29240
	Avg SP	200	18.9450	3.42353
	Low SP	250	19.6560	4.17701
	Total	847	19.1240	4.07871
Emotional	High SP	397	13.6272	7.01348
	Avg SP	200	15.5650	6.31229
	Low SP	250	16.8800	5.83247
	Total	847	15.0449	6.66421
Total Ajustment	High SP	397	55.8715	16.22883
	Avg SP	200	60.7700	14.84584
	Low SP	250	65.9280	15.72309
	Total	847	59.9965	16.32208

Table 4.53: Shows Tukey's Multiple Comparison HSD Test Showing Group Differences on Adjustment

Dependent Variable	(I) SP Level	(J) SP Level	Mean Difference (I-J)	Std. Error	Sig.	95% Confidence Interval	
						Lower Bound	Upper Bound
Home	High SP	AVG SP	-1.60298(*)	.41825	.000	-2.5850	-.6210
		Low SP	-2.91398(*)	.38944	.000	-3.8283	-1.9996
	Avg SP	Low SP	-1.31100(*)	.45759	.012	-2.3854	-.2366
Health	High SP	AVG SP	-1.29178(*)	.50856	.030	-2.4858	-.0978
		Low SP	-3.11278(*)	.47353	.000	-4.2246	-2.0010
	Avg SP	Low SP	-1.82100(*)	.55640	.003	-3.1273	-.5147
Social	High SP	AVG SP	-.06591	.35282	.981	-.8943	.7625
		Low SP	-.77691(*)	.32852	.048	-1.5482	-.0056
	Avg SP	Low SP	-.71100	.38601	.157	-1.6173	.1953
Emotional	High SP	AVG SP	-1.93780(*)	.56536	.002	-3.2652	-.6104
		Low SP	-3.25280(*)	.52642	.000	-4.4888	-2.0168
	Avg SP	Low SP	-1.31500	.61854	.085	-2.7672	.1372
Ajustment	High SP	AVG SP	-4.89846(*)	1.36684	.001	-8.1076	-1.6893
		Low SP	-10.05646(*)	1.27271	.000	-13.0446	-7.0683
	Avg SP	Low SP	-5.15800(*)	1.49542	.002	-8.6690	-1.6470

* = 0.05, ** = 0.01 significant level

Table 4.53 indicates that three groups namely: *(i)* high, *(ii)* average and *(iii)* low has been made on the basis of scores obtained by the adolescents on their perception about academic climate and efforts has been made for multiple comparison among these three groups on adjustment and its four areas.

Table 4.53 indicates that mean difference on following pairs found significant. On home adjustment high and average group (I-J=1.60), high and low (I-J=2.91) average and low (I-J=1.31), on health adjustment, high and average group (I-J=1.29), high and low (I-J=3.11) average and low (I-J=1.82), on social adjustment high and low group (I-J=0.77), on emotional adjustment high and average group (I-J=1.94), high and low (I-J=3.25). On over all adjustment high and average group (I-J=4.89), high and low (I- J=10.05), average and low group (I-J=5.16).

Hypothesis 25: There exists no significant effect of various levels of academic provisions (a dimensions of academic climate) on emotional intelligence.

Table 4.54: Shows Summary of one-way ANOVA on Emotional Intelligence

		Sum of Squares	df	Mean Squares	F	Sig.
Intra PA	Between Groups	248.985	2	124.493	9.936**	.000
	Within Groups	10575.303	845	12.530		
	Total	10824.288	847			
Inter PA	Between Groups	148.548	2	74.274	6.855**	.001
	Within Groups	9144.805	845	10.835		
	Total	9293.353	847			
Intra PM	Between Groups	374.612	2	187.306	13.506**	.000
	Within Groups	11704.817	845	13.868		
	Total	12079.429	847			
Inter PM	Between Groups	169.394	2	84.697	6.952**	.001
	Within Groups	10281.992	845	12.182		
	Total	10451.386	847			
EI	Between Groups	3476.628	2	1738.314	15.775**	.000
	Within Groups	93002.734	845	110.193		
	Total	96479.362	847			

* = 0.05, ** = 0.01 significant level

Table 4.54 indicates that high, average and low levels of academic provisions perceived by the adolescents are significantly differ on emotional intelligence and its four dimensions. It is found that three groups are significantly different on intrapersonal awareness (F=9.94,2,847; P<0.01), interpersonal awareness (F=6.86,2,847; P<0.01), intrapersonal management (F=13.51,2,847; P<0.01), interpersonal management (F=6.95,2,847; P<0.01) and overall emotional intelligence (F=15.78,2,847; P<0.01).

It is observed that these groups of academic provisions (academic climate) are significantly different on emotional intelligence and its four dimensions. So null hypothesis No. 25 is strongly rejected.

Table 4.55: Mean, SD and Number for Adolescents with High, Average and low Academic Provisions on Various Dimensions of Emotional Intelligence (N = 847)

EI Dimensions	Academic Provisions	N	Mean	SD
Intrapersonal Awareness	High AP	435	15.7908	3.47206
	Avg AP	267	14.7191	3.69512
	Low AP	145	14.6828	3.44743
	Total	847	15.2633	3.57696
Interpersonal Awareness	High AP	435	15.2552	3.20522
	Avg AP	267	14.4082	3.30897
	Low AP	145	14.4345	3.50954
	Total	847	14.8477	3.31437
Intrapersonal Management	High AP	435	18.4506	3.63790
	Avg AP	267	17.4494	3.77271
	Low AP	145	16.7517	3.88646
	Total	847	17.8442	3.77866
Interpersonal Management	High AP	435	17.2874	3.55765
	Avg AP	267	16.5281	3.55120
	Low AP	145	16.2138	3.15609
	Total	847	16.8642	3.51481
Total Emotional Intelligence	High AP	435	66.7609	10.19704
	Avg AP	267	63.1423	10.93601
	Low AP	145	62.0828	10.56166
	Total	847	64.8194	10.67904

Table 4.56: Shows Tukey's Multiple Comparison HSD Test Showing Group Differences on Emotional Intelligence and its Four Dimensions

Dependent Variable	(I) AP Level	(J) AP Level	Mean Difference (I-J)	Std. Error	Sig.	95% Confidence Interval	
						Lower Bound	Upper Bound
Intra PA	High AP	Avg AP	1.07170(*)	.27520	.000	.4256	1.7178
		Low AP	1.10805(*)	.33944	.003	.3111	1.9050
	Avg AP	Low AP	.03634	.36516	.995	-.8210	.8937
Inter PA	High AP	Avg AP	.84693(*)	.25591	.003	.2461	1.4478
		Low AP	.82069(*)	.31565	.026	.0796	1.5618
	Avg AP	Low AP	-.02624	.33957	.997	-.8235	.7710
Intra PM	High AP	Avg AP	1.00114(*)	.28952	.002	.3214	1.6809
		Low AP	1.69885(*)	.35711	.000	.8604	2.5373
	Avg AP	Low AP	.69771	.38417	.165	-.2043	1.5997
Inter PM	High AP	Avg AP	.75927(*)	.27135	.015	.1222	1.3964
		Low AP	1.07356(*)	.33470	.004	.2877	1.8594
	Avg AP	Low AP	.31430	.36006	.658	-.5311	1.1597
EI	High AP	Avg AP	3.61860(*)	.81610	.000	1.7025	5.5347
		Low AP	4.67816(*)	1.00661	.000	2.3148	7.0415
	Avg AP	Low AP	1.05956	1.08289	.591	-1.4829	3.6020

* = 0.05, ** = 0.01 significant level

In above Table 4.56, three groups (*e.g., (i)* high, *(ii)* average and *(iii)* low) has been made on the basis of scores obtained by the adolescents on their perception about academic climate (school provisions) and efforts has been made for multiple compression among these groups on emotional intelligence and its four dimensions.

Table 4.56 indicates that the mean differences of following pairs found significant. On intrapersonal awareness ,high, and average group (I-J=1.07), high and low (I-J=1.11), on interpersonal awareness high and average (I-J=.85), high and low (I-J=.82), on intrapersonal management, group high and average (I-J=1.00), high and low (I-J=1.69), on interpersonal management, group high and average (I-J=0.76), high and low (I-J=1.07), on emotional intelligence high and average (I-J=3.62), high and low (I-J=4.68) groups mean differences are significant.

Hypothesis No. 26: There exists no significant effect of various levels of academic provisions (a dimensions of academic climate) on adjustment.

Table 4.57: Shows Summary of one-way ANOVA on Adjustment
Academic Provisions (a dimensions of academic climate) (IV)

Adjustment (DV)		Sum of Squares	df	Mean Squares	F	Sig.
Home	Between Groups	566.492	2	283.246	11.715**	.000
	Within Groups	20406.990	845	24.179		
	Total	20973.483	847			
Health	Between Groups	388.674	2	194.337	5.444**	.004
	Within Groups	30130.183	845	35.699		
	Total	30518.857	847			
Social	Between Groups	57.127	2	28.563	1.720	.180
	Within Groups	14016.857	845	16.608		
	Total	14073.983	847			
Emotional	Between Groups	168.113	2	84.056	1.897	.151
	Within Groups	37404.182	845	44.318		
	Total	37572.295	847			
Overall Ajustment	Between Groups	4085.942	2	2042.971	7.792**	.000
	Within Groups	221297.047	845	262.200		
	Total	225382.989	847			

* = 0.05, ** = 0.01 significant level

Table 4.57 indicates that high, average and low levels of academic provisions by the adolescents are significantly differ on adjustment and its some areas. It is seen that three groups are significantly different on home adjustment (F=11.72,2,847; P<0.01) and health adjustment (F=5.44,2,847; P<0.01) and over all adjustment (F=7.92,2,847; P<0.01). However these groups are not different on social and emotional adjustment. So null hypothesis is partially accepted.

Table 4.58: Mean, SD and Number for Adolescents with High, Average and low Academic Provisions on Various Areas of Adjustment (N = 847)

Adjustment Areas	Academic Provision	N	• Mean	SD
Home	High AP	435	14.0483	4.76014
	Avg AP	267	15.5955	4.98883
	Low AP	145	15.8276	5.23920
	Total	847	14.8406	4.97909
Health	High AP	435	10.3333	5.49584
	Avg AP	267	11.5843	6.33253
	Low AP	145	11.8483	6.64301
	Total	847	10.9870	6.00619
Social	High AP	435	18.8713	3.94805
	Avg AP	267	19.3858	4.14006
	Low AP	145	19.4000	4.32435
	Total	847	19.1240	4.07871
Emotional	High AP	435	14.6115	6.76521
	Avg AP	267	15.5169	6.63117
	Low AP	145	15.4759	6.37060
	Total	847	15.0449	6.66421
Total Ajustment	High AP	435	57.8644	15.46417
	Avg AP	267	62.0824	17.09221
	Low AP	145	62.5517	16.62492
	Total	847	59.9965	16.32208

Table 4.59: Shows Tukey's Multiple Comparison HSD Test Showing Group Differences on Adjustment

Dependent Variable	(I) AP Level	(J) AP Level	Mean Difference (I-J)	Std. Error	Sig.	95% Confidence Interval	
						Lower Bound	Upper Bound
Home	High AP	Avg AP	-1.54723(*)	.38228	.000	-2.4448	-.6497
		Low AP	-1.77931(*)	.47152	.001	-2.8864	-.6722
	Avg AP	Low AP	-.23208	.50726	.891	-1.4230	.9589
Health	High AP	Avg AP	-1.25094(*)	.46451	.020	-2.3415	-.1603
		Low AP	-1.51494(*)	.57295	.023	-2.8601	-.1697
	Avg AP	Low AP	-.26401	.61637	.904	-1.7111	1.1831
Social	High AP	Avg AP	-.51450	.31683	.236	-1.2584	.2294
		Low AP	-.52874	.39079	.366	-1.4462	.3888
	Avg AP	Low AP	-.01423	.42040	.999	-1.0013	.9728
Emotional	High AP	Avg AP	-.90536	.51756	.188	-2.1205	.3098
		Low AP	-.86437	.63837	.366	-2.3632	.6344
	Avg AP	Low AP	.04099	.68675	.998	-1.5714	1.6534
Ajustment	High AP	Avg AP	-4.21803(*)	1.25888	.002	-7.1737	-1.2624
		Low AP	-4.68736(*)	1.55275	.007	-8.3330	-1.0417
	Avg AP	Low AP	-.46933	1.67042	.957	-4.3912	3.4526

* = 0.05, ** = 0.01 significant level

Table 4.59 indicates that three groups namely: *(i)* high, *(ii)* average and *(iii)* low has been made on the basis of scores obtained by the adolescents on their perception about academic climate and efforts has been made for multiple comparison among these three groups on adjustment and it's four areas.

Table 4.59 shows that the mean differences of following pairs found significant. On home adjustment high and average group (I-J=1.55) high and low group (I-J=1.78) on health adjustment, high and average group (I-J=1.25) high and low group (I-J=1.51), on over all adjustment high and average group (I-J=4.22), high and low (I-J=4.69). However no any significant difference found on social and emotional adjustment in three groups.

Hypothesis No. 27: There exists no significant effect of various levels of academic climate on emotional intelligence.

Table 4.60: Shows Summary of one-way ANOVA on Emotional Intelligence

Academic Climate (IV)

EI (DV)		Sum of Squares	df	Mean Squares	F	Sig.
Intra PA	Between Groups	662.294	2	331.147	27.503**	.000
	Within Groups	10161.994	845	12.040		
	Total	10824.288	847			
Inter PA	Between Groups	541.154	2	270.577	26.093**	.000
	Within Groups	8752.199	845	10.370		
	Total	9293.353	847			
Intra PM	Between Groups	1002.655	2	501.328	38.199**	.000
	Within Groups	11076.773	845	13.124		
	Total	12079.429	847			
Inter PM	Between Groups	536.206	2	268.103	22.821**	.000
	Within Groups	9915.180	845	11.748		
	Total	10451.386	847			
EI	Between Groups	10819.880	2	5409.940	53.304**	.000
	Within Groups	85659.482	845	101.492		
	Total	96479.362	847			

* = 0.05, ** = 0.01 significant level

Table 4.60 indicates that high, average and low levels of academic climate perceived by the adolescents are significantly differ on emotional intelligence its four dimensions. It is found that these groups are significantly different on intrapersonal awareness (F=27.50,2,847; P<0.01), interpersonal awareness (F=26.09,2,847; P<0.01) intrapersonal management (F=38.19, 2,847; P<0.01) interpersonal management (F=22.82, 2,847; P<0.01) and total emotional intelligence (F=53.30,2,847; P<0.01).

It is observed that three groups are significantly different on emotional intelligence and its four dimensions. So null hypothesis No. 27 is strongly rejected.

Table 4.61: Mean, SD and Number for Adolescents with High, Average and low Overall Academic Climate on Various Dimensions of Emotional Intelligence (N = 847)

EI Dimensions	Overall Academic Climate	N	Mean	SD
Intrapersonal Awareness	High ACL	405	16.0074	3.44798
	Avg ACL	232	15.2716	3.39205
	Low ACL	210	13.8190	3.59500
	Total	847	15.2633	3.57696
Interpersonal Awareness	High ACL	405	15.5160	3.25529
	Avg ACL	232	14.8664	3.17380
	Low ACL	210	13.5381	3.20302
	Total	847	14.8477	3.31437
Intrapersonal Management	High ACL	405	18.7012	3.70738
	Avg ACL	232	18.0000	3.19361
	Low ACL	210	16.0190	3.89327
	Total	847	17.8442	3.77866
Interpersonal Management	High ACL	405	17.5309	3.45153
	Avg ACL	232	16.8793	3.62209
	Low ACL	210	15.5619	3.14840
	Total	847	16.8642	3.51481
Total Emotional Intelligence	High ACL	405	67.7802	10.32437
	Avg ACL	232	64.9741	9.95571
	Low ACL	210	58.9381	9.70872
	Total	847	64.8194	10.67904

Table 4.62: Shows Tukey's Multiple Comparison HSD Test Showing Group Differences on Emotional Intelligence and its Four Dimensions

Dependent Variable	(I) ACL Total Level	(J) ACL Total Level	Mean Difference (I-J)	Std. Error	Sig.	95% Confidence Interval	
						Lower Bound	Upper Bound
Intra PA	High ACL	Avg ACL	.73586(*)	.28570	.027	.0651	1.4066
		Low ACL	2.18836(*)	.29507	.000	1.4956	2.8811
	Avg ACL	Low ACL	1.45250(*)	.33050	.000	.6765	2.2285
Inter PA	High ACL	Avg ACL	.64967(*)	.26515	.038	.0271	1.2722
		Low ACL	1.97795(*)	.27383	.000	1.3350	2.6209
	Avg ACL	Low ACL	1.32828(*)	.30672	.000	.6081	2.0484
Intra PM	High ACL	Avg ACL	.70123(*)	.29829	.050	.0009	1.4016
		Low ACL	2.68219(*)	.30806	.000	1.9589	3.4055
	Avg ACL	Low ACL	1.98095(*)	.34506	.000	1.1708	2.7911
Inter PM	High ACL	Avg ACL	.65155	.28221	.055	-.0110	1.3141
		Low ACL	1.96896(*)	.29146	.000	1.2847	2.6533
	Avg ACL	Low ACL	1.31741(*)	.32646	.000	.5509	2.0839
EI	High ACL	Avg ACL	2.80611(*)	.82950	.002	.8586	4.7536
		Low ACL	8.84215(*)	.85668	.000	6.8308	10.8535
	Avg ACL	Low ACL	6.03604(*)	.95956	.000	3.7831	8.2890

* = 0.05, ** = 0.01 significant level

Table 4.62 shows that three groups (*e.g.*, *(i)* high, *(ii)* average and *(iii)* low) has been made on the basis of scores obtained by the adolescents on their perception about academic climate and efforts has been made for multiple compression among these groups on emotional intelligence and its four dimensions.

Table 4.62 indicates that mean difference of following pairs found significant. On intrapersonal awareness, high, and average group (I-J=0.74), high and low (I-J=2.19), on average and low (I-J=1.33), on intrapersonal management, group high and average (I-J=0.70), high and low (I-J=2.68), on average and low (I-J=1.98), on emotional intelligence group high and average (I-J=2.80), high and low (I-J=8.84) and average and low group (I-J=6.04) mean differences are significant.

Hypothesis No. 28: There exists no significant effect of various levels of academic climate on adjustment.

Table 4.63: Shows Summary of one-way ANOVA on Adjustment

Academic Climate (IV)

Adjustment (DV)		Sum of Squares	df	Mean Squares	F	Sig.
Home	Between Groups	1228.619	2	614.309	26.259**	.000
	Within Groups	19744.864	845	23.394		
	Total	20973.483	847			
Health	Between Groups	1243.606	2	621.803	17.926**	.000
	Within Groups	29275.251	845	34.686		
	Total	30518.857	847			
Social	Between Groups	45.995	2	22.997	1.384	.251
	Within Groups	14027.989	845	16.621		
	Total	14073.983	847			
Emotional	Between Groups	1185.053	2	592.527	13.744**	.000
	Within Groups	36387.242	845	43.113		
	Total	37572.295	847			
Ajustment	Between Groups	12261.995	2	6130.997	24.280**	.000
	Within Groups	213120.994	845	252.513		
	Total	225382.989	847			

* = 0.05, ** = 0.01 significant level

Table 4.63 indicates that high, average and low levels of academic climate by the adolescents are significantly differ on adjustment and its some areas. It is seen that three groups are significantly different on home adjustment (F=26.26,2,847; P<0.01) and health adjustment (F=17.93,2,847; P<0.01), emotional adjustment (F=13.74,2,847; P<0.01) and over all adjustment (F=24.28,2,847; P<0.01). However, no any significant difference found in these groups on social adjustment. So null hypothesis is rejected.

Table 4.64: Mean, SD and Number for Adolescents with High, Average and low Overall Academic Climate on Various Areas of Adjustment (N = 847)

Adjustment Areas	Overall Academic Climate	N	Mean	SD
Home	High ACL	405	13.7086	4.84758
	Avg ACL	232	15.1853	4.67980
	Low ACL	210	16.6429	4.98429
	Total	847	14.8406	4.97909
Health	High ACL	405	9.9407	5.66747
	Avg ACL	232	11.0474	5.60862
	Low ACL	210	12.9381	6.57391
	Total	847	10.9870	6.00619
Social	High ACL	405	18.8815	4.12080
	Avg ACL	232	19.3190	3.84347
	Low ACL	210	19.3762	4.23885
	Total	847	19.1240	4.07871
Emotional	High ACL	405	13.9778	6.99873
	Avg ACL	232	15.2371	6.68977
	Low ACL	210	16.8905	5.47307
	Total	847	15.0449	6.66421
Total Ajustment	High ACL	405	56.5086	6.09911
	Avg ACL	232	60.7888	16.30906
	Low ACL	210	65.8476	14.99109
	Total	847	59.9965	16.32208

Table 4.65: Shows Tukey's Multiple Comparison HSD Test Showing Group Differences on Adjustment and it's Four Areas

Dependent Variable	(I) ACL Total Level	(J) ACL Total Level	Mean Difference (I-J)	Std. Error	Sig.	95% Confidence Interval	
						Lower Bound	Upper Bound
Home	High ACL	Avg ACL	-1.47670(*)	.39825	.001	-2.4117	-.5417
		Low ACL	-2.93422(*)	.41130	.000	-3.8999	-1.9685
	Avg ACL	Low ACL	-1.45751(*)	.46069	.005	-2.5392	-.3759
Health	High ACL	Avg ACL	-1.10667	.48493	.059	-2.2452	.0319
		Low ACL	-2.99735(*)	.50082	.000	-4.1732	-1.8215
	Avg ACL	Low ACL	-1.89068(*)	.56097	.002	-3.2077	-.5736
Social	High ACL	Avg ACL	-.43748	.33568	.394	-1.2256	.3506
		Low ACL	-.49471	.34668	.327	-1.3087	.3192
	Avg ACL	Low ACL	-.05722	.38831	.988	-.9689	.8545
Emotional	High ACL	Avg ACL	-1.25929	.54063	.052	-2.5286	.0100
		Low ACL	-2.91270(*)	.55835	.000	-4.2236	-1.6018
	Avg ACL	Low ACL	-1.65341(*)	.62540	.023	-3.1218	-.1851
Ajustment	High ACL	Avg ACL	-4.28015(*)	1.30840	.003	-7.3521	-1.2082
		Low ACL	-9.33898(*)	1.35127	.000	-12.5116	-6.1664
	Avg ACL	Low ACL	-5.05883(*)	1.51356	.002	-8.6124	-1.5052

* = 0.05, ** = 0.01 significant level

Table 4.65 indicates that three groups namely: *(i)* high, *(ii)* average and *(iii)* low has been made on the basis of scores obtained by the adolescents on their perception about academic climate and efforts has been made for multiple comparison among these three groups on adjustment and its four areas.

Table 4.65 shows that the mean differences of following pairs found significant. On home adjustment high and average group (I-J=1.48), high and low group (I-J=2.93), average and low group (I-J=1.46), on health adjustment, high and low group (I-J=2.99) average and low group (I-J=1.89), on emotional adjustment, high and low group (I-J=2.91), average and low (I-J=1.65) and over all adjustment high and average group (I-J=4.28), high and low (I-J=9.34), average and low (I-J=5.06).

Hypothesis No. 29: Parental acceptance attitude and academic climate will be jointly and significantly interact to yield different outcomes of emotional intelligence.

Table 4.66: Shows Summary of two-way ANOVA on Emotional Intelligence

Dependent Variable: EI

Source of Variance	Sum of Squares	df	Mean Squares	F	Sig.
Parental Acceptance	814.561	2	407.280	4.070	.017*
Academic Climate	7065.828	2	3532.914	35.306	.000**
Parental Acceptance X Academic Climate	607.030	5	151.757	1.517	NS
Error Variance	83854.183	838	100.065		
Total	3655192.00	847			

* = 0.05, ** = 0.01 significant level

In the present study it was hypothesized that parental acceptance attitude and academic climate will be jointly and significantly interact to yield different outcomes of emotional intelligence. To test this hypothesis the two way ANOVA was performed. The parental acceptance and academic climate are independent variables while emotional intelligence is dependent variable.

It is noticed from Table 4.66, that the main effect of parental acceptance (F=4.00, 2,838; P<0.01) is significant. It means that different levels of parental acceptance create different output of emotional intelligence among adolescents. It is also seen that the main effect of academic climate found statistically significant (F=35.31, 2,838; P<0.01) on emotional intelligence of adolescents. However interaction effect of these independent variables found no significant (F=1.52, 2,838; P>0.05).

Table 4.67: Shows Scheffe's Multiple Comparison Test Showing Group Differences on Emotional Intelligence

Dependent Variable: EI

(I) Parental Acceptance	(J) Parental Acceptance	Mean Difference (I-J)	Std. Error	Sig.	95% Confidence Interval	
					Lower Bound	Upper Bound
High PA	Avg PA	2.3130(*)	.76807	.011	.4296	4.1964
	Low PA	5.7188(*)	.98798	.000	3.2961	8.1414
Avg PA	Low PA	3.4057(*)	.94695	.002	1.0837	5.7278

* = 0.05, ** = 0.01 significant level

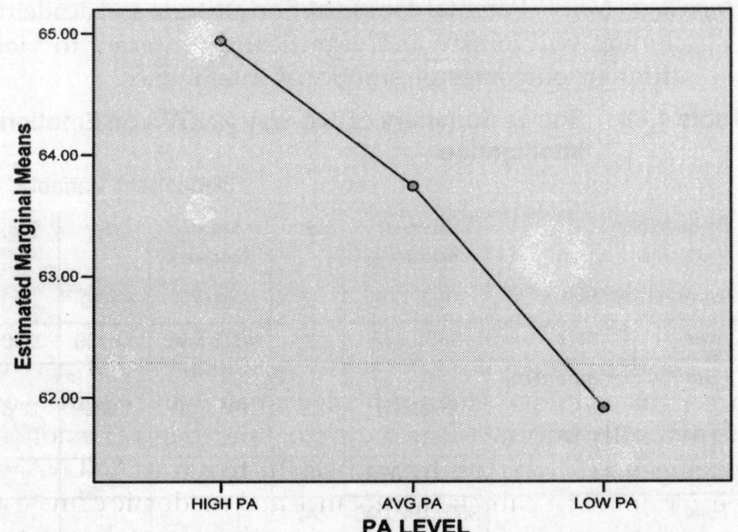

Fig. 4.1: Parental Acceptance and Emotional Intelligence

Table 4.67 indicates that three groups namely, high average and low has been made on the basis of scores obtained by the adolescents on their perception about their parental acceptance attitude and efforts has been made for multiple comparison among these three groups on emotional intelligence.

Table 4.67 indicates the mean difference of following pairs found significant on emotional intelligence. Group high and average (I-J=2.31), high and low group (I-J=5.72) and average and low (I-J=3.40) on the whole results indicates that there is significant difference between high, average and low groups of parental acceptance attitude on emotional intelligence.

Table 4.67 presents the results of post hoc analysis which reveals significant decrease in scores of emotional intelligence from high, average and low levels of parental acceptance attitude. The results are further highlighted in the Figure 4.1. This reduction of emotional intelligence score might be due to the effectiveness of parental acceptance attitude. Those parents accept their children on high level they shows more emotional intelligence. On the contrary low accepted adolescents showed low emotional intelligence.

Hypothesis No. 30: Parental concentration attitude and academic climate will jointly and significantly interact to yield different outcomes of emotional intelligence.

Table 4.68: Shows Summary of two-way ANOVA on Emotional Intelligence

Dependent Variable: EI

Source of Variance	Sum of Squares	df	Mean Squares	F	Sig.
Parental Concentration	1696.005	2	848.003	8.529	.000
Academic Climate	8631.252	2	4315.626	43.406	.000
Parental Concentration X Academic Climate	405.275	5	101.319	1.019	.396
Error Variance	83317.098	838	99.424		
Total	3655192.000	847			

* = 0.05, ** = 0.01 significant level

It is noticed from Table 4.68, that the main effect of parental concentration (F=8.53, 2,838; P<0.01) is significant. It means that different levels of parental concentration attitude create different outputs of emotional intelligence among adolescents. It is also observed that the main effect of academic climate found significant (F=43.41, 2,838: P<0.01) on emotional intelligence. However, interaction effect of parental concentration and academic climate found no significant (F=1.02, 2,838; P>0.05).

Table 4.69: Shows Seheffe's Multiple Comparison Test Showing Group Difference on Emotional Intelligence

Dependent Variable: Emotional Intelligence

(I) Parental Acceptance Concentration	(J) Parental Acceptance Concentration	Mean Difference (I-J)	Std. Error	Sig.	95% Confidence Interval	
					Lower Bound	Upper Bound
High PC	Avg PC	-2.0681(*)	.79499	.034	-4.0175	-.1186
	Low PC	-4.3523(*)	.93864	.000	-6.6540	-2.0507
Avg PC	Low PC	-2.2842(*)	.87493	.034	-4.4297	-.1388

* = 0.05, ** = 0.01 significant level

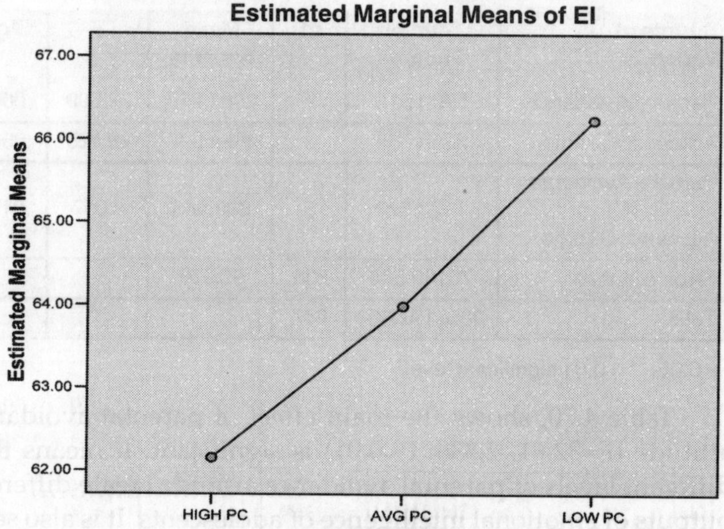

Fig. 4.2: Parental Concentration and Emotional Intelligence

Table 4.69 indicates that there are three groups has been made on the basis of scores obtained by the adolescents on their perception about their parental concentration attitude and effort has been made multiple comparison among these three groups on EI.

Table 4.69 indicates that mean difference on following pairs found significant on EI. Group high and average (I-J=2.07), high and low (I-J=4.35), average and low (I-J=2.28). Whole result showed that there is significant difference among these groups of parental concentration on EI of adolescents. The results are further depicted in the Figure 4.2. High parental concentration attitude creates low emotional intelligence, on the contrary low parental concentration attitude results high EI.

Hypothesis: No. 31: Parental avoidance attitude and academic climate will jointly and significantly interact to yield different outcomes of emotional intelligence.

Table 4.70: Shows Summary of two-way ANOVA on Emotional Intelligence

Dependent Variable: EI

Source of Variance	Sum of Squares	df	Mean Squares	F	Sig.
Parental Avoidance	5929.518	2	2964.759	32.609	.000
Academic Climate	5368.755	2	2684.377	29.525	.000
Parental Avoidance X Academic Climate	1122.570	5	280.643	3.087	.015
Error Variance	76189.546	838	90.918		
Total	3655192.000	847			

* = 0.05, ** = 0.01 significant level

Table 4.70, shows the main effect of parental avoidance attitude (F=32.61, 2,838; P<0.01) is significant. It means that different levels of parental avoidance attitude create different outputs of emotional intelligence of adolescents. It is also seen that main effect of academic climate is significant (F=29.53, 2,

838, P<0.01). But interaction effect of PV and academic climate found non-significant.

Table 4.71: Shows Seheffe's Multiple Comparison Test Showing Group Difference on Emotional Intelligence

Dependent Variable: EI

(I) Parental Acceptance Aviodance	(J) Parental Acceptance Aviodance	Mean Difference (I-J)	Std. Error	Sig.	95% Confidence Interval	
					Lower Bound	Upper Bound
High PV	Avg PV	-4.0574(*)	.79200	.000	-5.9995	-2.1153
	Low PV	-9.7448(*)	.79832	.000	-11.7024	-7.7872
Avg PV	Low PV	-5.6874(*)	.82227	.000	-7.7037	-3.6711

* = 0.05, ** = 0.01 significant level

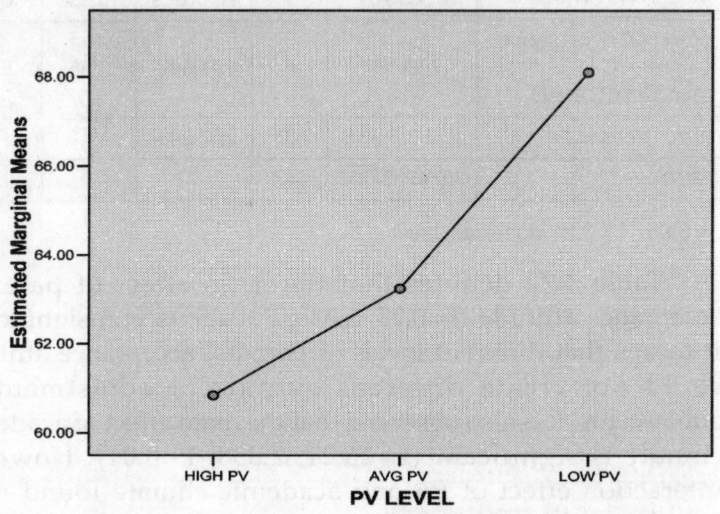

Fig. 4.3: Parental Avoidance and Emotional Intelligence

Table 4.71 indicates that mean differences on following pairs found significant on EI. Group high and average (I-J=4.06), high and low (I-J=9.74) average and low (I-J=5.69). It is found that there is significant difference among three groups of parental avoidance on EI, of adolescents. The results are further depicted in Figure 4.3. It is interpreted that high parental avoidance attitude create low emotional intelligence and parental low avoidance attitude develops high emotional intelligence in adolescents.

Hypothesis: No. 32: Parental acceptance attitude and academic climate will jointly and significantly interact to yield different outcomes of adjustment.

Table 4.72: Shows Summary of two-way ANOVA on Adjustment Tests of between-Subjects Effects

Dependent Variable: Ajustment

Source of Variance	Sum of Squares	df	Mean Squares	F	Sig.
Parental Acceptance	115.712	2	57.856	.228	.796
Academic Climate	8223.737	2	4111.869	16.237	.000
Parental Acceptance X Academic Climate	766.197	5	191.549	.756	.554
Error Variance	212217.985	838	253.243		
Total	3274223.000	847			

* = 0.05, ** = 0.01 significant level

Table 4.72 denotes that the main effect of parental acceptance attitude (F=0.23, 2,838; P>0.05) is non-significant. It means that different levels of parental acceptance attitude could not create different outputs of adjustment of adolescents. It is also observed that the main effect of academic climate is significant (F=16.24, 2,838; P<0.01). However interaction effect of PA and academic climate found non-significant.

Table 4.73 shows the difference of three pairs found non-significant. It means that there is no significant difference among three groups of parental acceptance on adjustment of adolescents.

Table 4.73 Shows Seheffe's Multiple Comparison test Showing Group Difference on Adjustment

Dependent Variable: Ajustment

(I) Parental Acceptance	(J) Parental Acceptance	Mean Difference (I-J)	Std. Error	Sig.	95% Confidence Interval	
					Lower Bound	Upper Bound
High PA	Avg PA	-.2563	1.22188	.978	-3.2525	2.7400
	Low PA	-3.0412	1.57173	.154	-6.8953	.8128
Avg PA	Low PA	-2.7850	1.50645	.182	-6.4790	.9090

* = 0.05, ** = 0.01 significant level

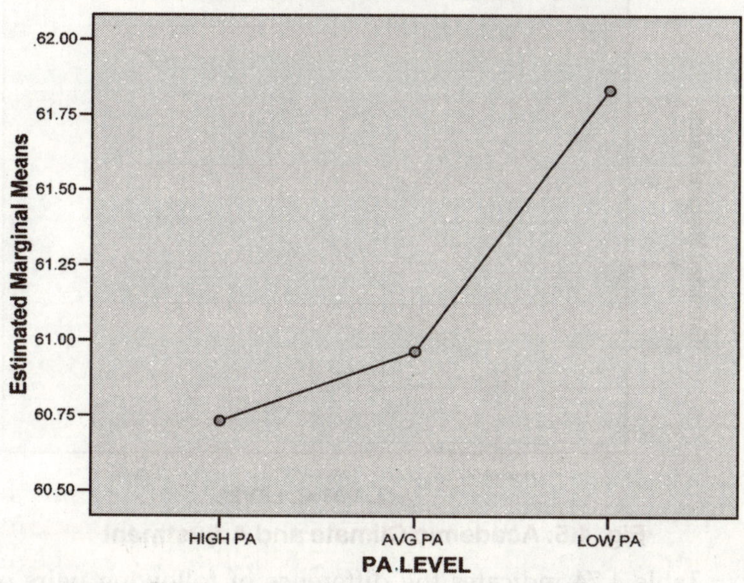

Fig. 4.4: Parental Acceptance and Adjustment

The results of further depicted in Figure 4.4. It is observed that high parental acceptance attitude create satisfactory adjustment of adolescent on the contrary low parental acceptance attitude results poor adjustment of adolescents.

Table 4.74: Shows Scheffe's Multiple Comparisons Test Showing Group Difference on Adjustment

Dependent Variable: Ajustment

(I) Academic Climate	(J) Academic Climate	Mean Difference (I-J)	Std. Error	Sig.	95% Confidence Interval	
					Lower Bound	Upper Bound
High ACL	Avg ACL	-4.2802(*)	1.31029	.005	-7.4931	-1.0672
	Low ACL	-9.3390(*)	1.35322	.000	-12.6573	-6.0207
Avg ACL	Low ACL	-5.0588(*)	1.51575	.004	-8.7756	-1.3420

* = 0.05, ** = 0.01 significant level

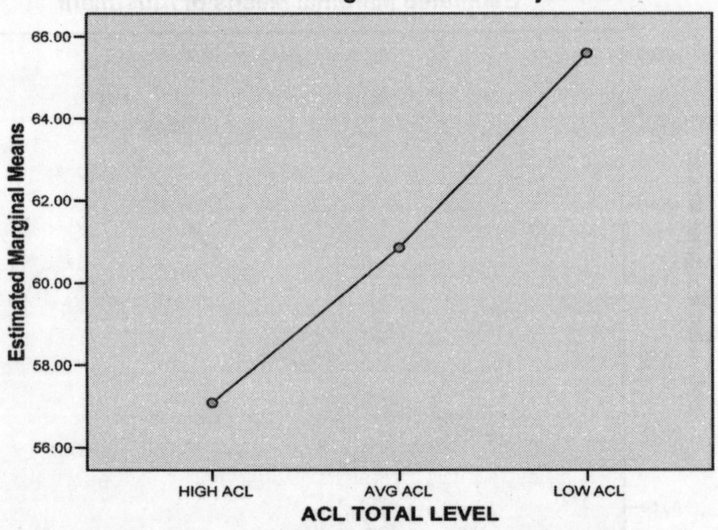

Fig. 4.5: Academic Climate and Adjustment

Table 4.74 indicates the difference of following pairs of academic climate found significant on adjustment. Group high and average (I-J=4.28), high and low (I-J=9.33), average and low (I-J=5.06). It means that there is significant difference among three groups of academic climate on adjustment. This result is depicted in Figure 4.5. The graph shows that high academic climate creates good adjustment of adolescents and low academic climate poor adjustment of adolescents.

Hypothesis: No. 33: Parental concentration attitude and academic climate will jointly and significantly interact to yield different outcomes of adjustment.

Table 4.75: Shows Summary of two-way ANOVA on Adjustment Tests of Between-Subjects Effects

Dependent Variable: Ajustment

Source of Variance	Sum of Squares	df	Mean Squares	F	Sig.
Parental Concentration	13317.043	2	6658.521	28.221	.000
Academic Climate	9113.043	2	4556.521	19.312	.000
Parental Concentration X Academic Climate	923.587	5	230.897	.979	.418
Error Variance	197716.347	838	235.938		
Total	3274223.000	847			

* = 0.05, ** = 0.01 significant level

Table 4.75 indicates that the main effect of parental concentration attitude (F=28.28, 2,838; P<0.01) is significant. It means that different levels of parental concentration attitude create different output of adjustment. It is also seen that the main effect of academic climate is significant (F=19.31, 2,838; P<0.01). But interaction effect of parental concentration and academic climate is non-significant.

Table 4.76: Shows Scheff's Multiple Comparison Test Showing Group Difference on Adjustment

Dependent Variable: Ajustment

(I) Parental Concentr-ation	(J) Parental Concentr-ation	Mean Difference (I-J)	Std. Error	Sig.	95% Confidence Interval	
					Lower Bound	Upper Bound
High PC	Avg PC	7.3645(*)	1.22467	.000	4.3615	10.3676
	Low PC	10.9092(*)	1.44594	.000	7.3636	14.4549
Avg PC	Low PC	3.5447(*)	1.34781	.032	.2397	6.8497

* = 0.05, ** = 0.01 significant level

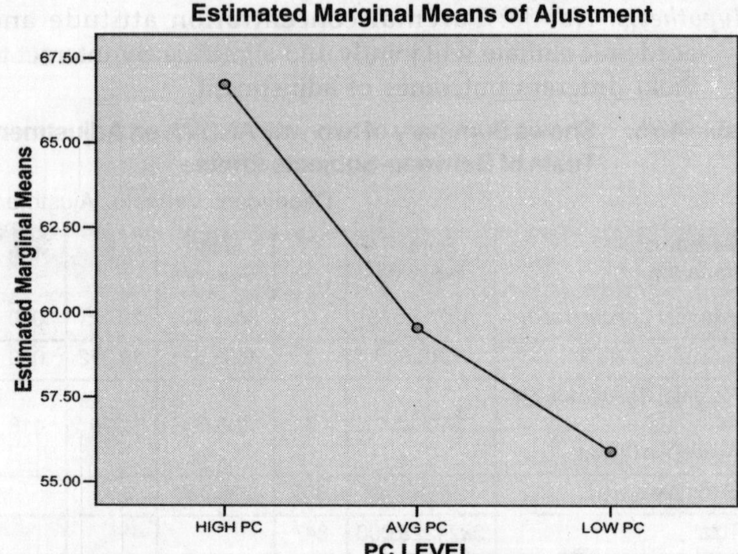

Fig 4.6: Parental Concentration and Adjustment

Table 4.76 indicates that the following pairs found significant difference. Group high and average (I-J=7.4) high and low (I-J=10.91), average and low (I-J=3.54). It means that there is significant difference among three groups of parental concentration on adjustment. The results are further depicted in Figure 4.6. It is interpreted that high parental concentration results poor adjustment of adolescents. On the contrary low and average parental concentration attitude creates good adjustment in adolescents.

Hypothesis: No. 34: Parental avoidance attitude and academic climate will jointly and significantly interact to yield different outcomes of adjustment.

Table 4.77 indicates that the main effect of parental avoidance attitude (F=61.33, 2,838; P<0.01) is significant. It means that there are different outputs of adjustment among adolescents. It is observed that the main effect of academic climate found significant (F=5.37, 2,838; P<0.01) on adjustment. However, interaction effect of parental avoidance and academic climate found non-significant (F=1.85, 2, 838, P>0.05).

Table 4.77: Shows Summary of two-way ANOVA on Adjustment Tests of Between-Subjects Effects

Dependent Variable: Ajustment

Source of Variance	Sum of Square	df	Mean Square	F	Sig.
Parental Avoidance	26730.647	2	13365.324	61.329	.000
Academic Climate	2342.482	2	1171.241	5.374	.005
Parental Avoidance X Academic Climate	1612.333	5	403.083	1.850	.117
Error Variance	182624.923	838	217.930		
Total	3274223.000	847			

*= 0.05, ** = 0.01 significant level

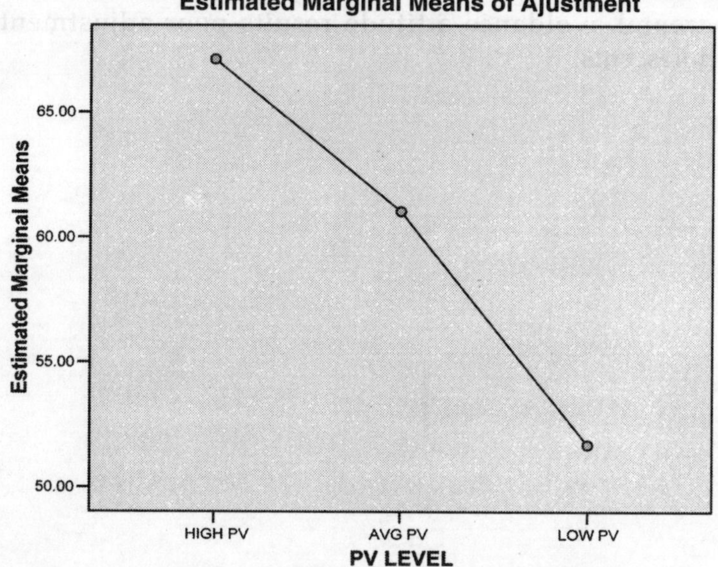

Fig. 4.7: Parental Avoidance Attitude and Adjustment

Table 4.78 indicates that the following pairs found significant difference. Group high and average (I-J=7.51), high and low (I-J=16.29) average and low (I-J=8.77). It means that there is significant difference among three groups of parental

Table 4.78: Shows Scheff's Multiple Comparison Test Showing Group Difference on Adjustment

Dependent Variable: Ajustment

(I) Parental Avoidance	(J) Parental Avoidance	Mean Difference (I-J)	Std. Error	Sig.	95% Confidence Interval	
					Lower Bound	Upper Bound
High PV	Avg PV	7.5146(*)	1.22619	.000	4.5078	10.5213
	Low PV	16.2881(*)	1.23598	.000	13.2574	19.3189
Avg PV	Low PV	8.7736(*)	1.27305	.000	5.6519	11.8953

* = 0.05, ** = 0.01 significant level

avoidance on adjustment. The results are further depicted in Figure 4.7. It is interpreted that high parental avoidance attitude create poor adjustment of adolescent whereas low parental avoidance attitude results poor adjustment of adolescents.

5 DISCUSSION

It is essential to retrospect the aim and objectives of the research before discussing the results which were obtained from the collected data and its analysis. The main aim of the study was to find out the effect of family relationship and academic climate on emotional intelligence and adjustment of adolescents. This chapter attempts to discuss in detail, the relevant findings depicted in the previous chapter in the light of relevant literature.

The first hypothesis was stated that 'Male and female adolescents would not on differ their mothers and fathers (parental) acceptance attitude.'

This hypothesis is strongly accepted in the present study. The results show that male and female adolescents are not significantly differ on parental acceptance attitude. Previous study of Fatos Erkman and Aysen Ekmekei (2011) found that overall children perceived their fathers in a more positive way than they did their mothers. They also found that the low level of agreement between children's and mothers' as well as between children's and fathers' reports of acceptance and behavioural control.

Second hypothesis was framed that, 'There will be no significant difference between male and female adolescents on their mothers and fathers concentration attitude.' This hypothesis is partly accepted. It is found that fathers are more concentrating on their male adolescent children. In the study of Fatos Erkman and Aysen Ekmekei (2011) found that overall children perceived their fathers in a more positive way than their mothers. In Indian culture father is considers his son as a support of old age.

The hypothesis No. 3 'There will be no significant difference between male and female adolescents on their mothers and fathers (parental) avoidance attitude.' This hypothesis is rejected in the present study. The results found that there is a significant difference between male and female adolescents on their parental avoidance attitude. Mothers and fathers showed more avoidance attitude to males and females. Previous studies of Biradar Sweta (2006) found that 60 per cent of female respondent and about 51 per cent of male respondents had perceived that they were being rejected by their parents.

Fourth hypothesis was framed that 'There would be no significant difference between male and female adolescents' perception on various components of academic climate.' In the present study it is found that the perception of male and female adolescents is different regarding physical material, interpersonal trust, academic provisions and total academic climate. It is observed that female adolescent's perception of their academic climate is better than male adolescents. So null hypothesis is rejected. But in the previous research findings reported that perception of school climate are closely tied to various demographic variables such as gender and socio-economic status. Research has suggested that adolescent girls may experience school as a less supportive environment than boys, stemming from institutional gender biases and greater likelihood of sexual harassment from male peers.

It was hypothesized No. 5 that 'There will be no significant difference between male and female adolescents on various dimensions of emotional intelligence.' Present study found that there is significant difference between male and female adolescents on interpersonal management. It shows that female adolescents have more ability of interpersonal management than male adolescents. But regarding overall emotional intelligence there no significant difference found between male and female adolescents. Previous studies of Brackett and Mayer (2003) was mentioned the gender difference on emotional intelligence. But Schutte *et al*. (1998); Furnham (2000) did not find gender difference on emotional intelligence. Kaytal and Awasthi (2005) found that girls have more emotional intelligence than boys.

Sixth hypothesis was formed that 'There will be no significant difference between male and female adolescents on various areas of adjustment.' It is found that female adolescents have good adjustment in home and social areas. Males have good adjustment in emotional area. But there is no significant difference between male and female adolescents on overall adjustment. Previous research stated that boys and girls do not differ on their adjustment (Shahpur, 2004). Rather (1990) found that girls were socially better adjusted than boys.

Hypothesis No. 7 was 'There will be no significant difference between urban and rural adolescents on their mothers and fathers (Parental) acceptance attitude.' Results show that there is no significant difference between urban and rural adolescents on their parental acceptance attitude. It means that area of residence could not affect on parental acceptance attitude. This urban life is fast and stressful as compared to rural life, parents of urban as well as rural area look after their children lovingly. So there is no difference in acceptance attitude of urban and rural parents.

It was hypothesized No. 8 that 'There will be no significant difference between urban and rural adolescents on their mothers and fathers (Parental) concentration attitude.' It is found that there is no significant difference between urban and rural adolescents on their mothers' concentration attitude. But fathers of rural area are more concentrating on their adolescents' children than urban fathers. This study also indicates that rural parents are more concentrating than urban parents to their adolescent children.

Hypothesis No. 9 was framed that 'There will be no significant difference between urban and rural adolescents on their mothers' and fathers' (parental) avoidance attitude.' This null hypothesis is rejected in present study. It is found that rural mothers and fathers avoid their adolescents children more than urban mothers and fathers.

The next hypothesis No. 10 was 'There would be no significant difference between urban and rural adolescents perception on their various dimensions of academic climate'. Results show that there in difference between urban and rural adolescents on school provisions and academic provisions. It is interpreted that rural adolescents feel that their schools are not providing school and academic facilities as compared to urban schools. However, there is no significant difference found between urban and rural adolescents perception on overall academic climate. Previous research of McEvoy and Welker (2000) reported that positive interpersonal relationships and optimum learning opportunities for students in all demographic environments can increase achievement level and reduce maladaptive behaviour. School climate can play a significant role in providing a healthy and positive school atmosphere.

Hypothesis No. 11 was 'There will be no significant difference between urban and rural adolescents on various dimension of emotional intelligence.' Results indicate that urban and rural adolescents have no significant difference on emotional intelligence. But previous research of Wing and Love (2001) reported that urban students had comparatively better emotional intelligence than rural students.

The hypothesis No. 12 was 'There will be no significant difference between urban and rural adolescents on various areas of adjustment. Results show that urban and rural adolescents are significantly different on home, health, social emotional and overall adjustment. It means that cultural difference can affect adolescents adjustment. Urban adolescents have better adjustment than rural adolescents. Previous research of Wing and Love (2001) supporting this findings. Shah (1989) also found that urban boys had better adjustment than rural boys.

The hypothesis No. 13 was framed that 'The various levels of parental acceptance attitude will yield different outcomes of emotional intelligence of adolescents.' Results indicate that, parental acceptance attitude three groups (*e.g.*, high, average and low) are significantly varied on intrapersonal awareness, intrapersonal management, interpersonal management and overall emotional intelligence. One way ANOVA was performed to find out the group difference on emotional intelligence of high, average and low parental acceptance attitude perceived by the adolescents.

One way ANOVA gives (Table 4.18) a global picture and tells that intergroup mean differences are significantly large or not, but it does not tell us whether group 1 *vs* group 2 or group 1 *vs* group 3 comparisons show significantly large mean difference or not. For this purpose in present study Tukey's multiple comparison HSD test has been employed.

Regarding Tukey's test, it is found that (Table 4.20) there is significant difference between high and low group of parental acceptance. It is noticed that all pairs of parental acceptance is significant on interpersonal management. When multiple comparison among three groups of parental acceptance attitude (PA) on overall emotional intelligence, it is seen that all pairs of PA are significant. It means parental acceptance attitude affects on emotional intelligence of adolescents. Previous researches support this finding. While parents' interaction with child and their form of attachment affect the emotional intelligence of child, home environment can be seen as a natural environment for the constitution of emotions and emotional attachment (Raikes, and Thompson, 2006). Umadevi and Rayal (2004) stated that the emotional intelligence of the child depends on parental love and affection and depending on the child rearing practices and interactions with them.

Hypothesis No. 14 was formulated that, 'There exists no significant difference in adjustment on various levels of parental acceptance of adolescents.' In Table 4.21 results depict that three groups of parental acceptance attitude (PA) are significantly varied on home adjustment at 0.01 level and social adjustment at 0.05 level. So null hypothesis is partially accepted.

As per Tukey's multiple comparison test mean difference found between high and low PA group and average and low group of PA. It is also noticed that mean difference between high and low PA on social adjustment. It is seen that mean differences of all pairs of PA are not significant on health, emotional and overall adjustment. It means that PA attitude affects on home and social adjustment of adolescents. If PA is high adjustment also high. Low PA creates poor adjustment in adolescents. Previous researches supporting this finding. Doyle and Moretti (2000) found that secure attachment continues to contribute to adjustment in adolescence. Dembo, Smau and Savin (1987) reported that good relation with parents tend to show better social adjustment.

Hypothesis No. 15, this hypothesis states that 'There exists no significant effect among levels of parental concentration on emotional intelligence (EI) of adolescents.' Table 4.24 shown in the previous chapter, it is quite clear that three groups (*e.g.*, high, average and low) of parental concentration (PC) attitude are significantly different on intrapersonal awareness, interpersonal awareness, interpersonal management and overall emotional intelligence. So hypothesis No. 15 is strongly rejected in present study.

Regarding Tukey's multiple comparison test the significant mean difference is found among PC on intrapersonal and interpersonal awareness Gr. high and average, Gr. high and low, Gr. average and low. On interpersonal management Gr. high and low found significant. On overall EI three groups significantly differ from each other. It is interpreted that high PC creates low EI and low PC helps for development of EI. Previous research supported this finding. Bhatia Gunjan (2012) reported that healthy family relationship greatly influences on EI of the adolescents.

It was hypothesized No. 16 that, 'There exists no significant effect of various levels of parental concentration (PC) attitude on adjustment of adolescents.'

Table 4.27 depicted in the previous chapter, it is seen that three groups of PC significantly differ on home, health, social, emotional and overall adjustment. So null hypothesis No. 16 strongly rejected in the study.

Regarding Tukey's multiple comparison test (Table 4.28) indicates that mean differences for all pairs of PC on adjustment and its four areas found significant. It means that high PC becomes the barrier in adjustment. But low and average PC supports the adolescents for adjustment. Previous research finding supported this research. Chakra and Prabha (2004) found that emotional and social adjustment of children was superior, who was loved, accepted and trusted by their parents.

Hypothesis No. 17 was formulated that 'There exists no significant effect on various levels of parental avoidance (PV) attitude on emotional intelligence and its four dimensions'.

Table 4.30 indicates that three groups of PV significantly differ on intrapersonal awareness, interpersonal awareness, intrapersonal management and interpersonal management and overall EI. So null hypothesis is strongly rejected.

As per Tukey's multiple comparison (Table 4.32), it is seen that mean difference in all pairs of PV on EI found significant. It means that high PV negatively influence on development of EI than average and low PV. Previous study supported this finding. Chopra and Nangru (2013) reported that parental avoidance has negative but significant relationship with EI.

In hypothesis No. 18 was stated that, 'There exists no significant effect of various levels of parental avoidance (PV) attitude on adjustment and its four areas'.

Regarding Table 4.33 depicted that three groups of PV significantly differ on home, health, social, emotional and overall adjustment. So null hypothesis No. 18 is strongly rejected.

In the Table No. 4.35 Tukey's multiple comparison test showed PV group differences on adjustment. The mean difference for all pairs of PV on adjustment and its four areas found significant. It means that high PV creates poor adjustment in adolescents. Previous research supported this finding. Jay and Sigh (1991) conducted a study on 'the role of parental rejection on the development of neuroses among adolescents. The sample consisted of 200 school going children and were classified as 100 most rejected and 100 most accepted. The parent – child relation questionnaire was used. The results revealed that the rejected children were more inclined towards neurotic tendencies.

Hypothesis No. 19 tated that, 'There exists no significant effect of various levels of physical material (PM) on emotional intelligence (EI).'

Table 4.36 indicates that three groups of PM (*e.g.*, high, average and low) perceived by the adolescents significantly differ on EI and its four dimensions. So null hypothesis is strongly rejected.

Table 4.38 Tukey's multiple comparison test showing PM group differences on EI and its four factors. The mean difference of high and average group and high and low group found significant. It is interpreted that those schools have lack of PM it affects on EI of adolescents.

Hypothesis No. 20 was formulated 'There exists no significant effect of various levels of physical material (PM) on adjustment.'

Table 4.39 indicates that three levels of PM (*e.g.*, high, average and low) perceived by the adolescents significantly affects home, health and overall adjustment. So null hypothesis is partially rejected.

Tukey's multiple comparison test shows PM group differences on home, health, emotional and overall adjustment. The mean difference of group high and average, high and low showed significant. It means that those schools providing good PM to their students, it is helpful to them to develop their EI.

In the hypothesis No. 21 stated that, 'There exists no significant effect of various levels of interpersonal trust (IPT) on emotional intelligence (EI).'

Table 4.42 mentioned that three levels of IPT perceived by the adolescents significantly affects on EI and its four dimensions. So null hypothesis is strongly rejected.

Table 4.44 Tukey's multiple comparison test shows IPT group difference on EI. The mean differences in group high and low, group high and average and group average and low on some factors of EI found significant differences. It means that where relationship between student-teacher, principal-teacher, teacher-teacher is healthy. It affects EI of adolescents. Previous research supported this finding. Manning and Saddlemire (1996) concluded that aspects of school climate including trust, respect, mutual obligation and concern for others welfare can have powerful effects on educators and learner's interpersonal relationship.

Hypothesis No. 22 was stated that, 'There exists no significant effect of various levels of interpersonal trust on adjustment.'

Table 4.45 showing that three levels of IPT perceived by the adolescents significantly affects home, health, emotional and overall adjustment. In Tukey's multiple comparison test observed IPT group difference on adjustment. It means that healthy relationships between teacher-student, teacher-teacher, principal-teacher it affects satisfactory adjustment of adolescents.

Hypothesis No. 23 was formulated that, 'There exists no significant effect of various levels of school provision (SP) on emotional intelligence (EI).'

Table 4.48 shows that three levels of SP perceived by the adolescents significantly affects EI and its four dimensions. So hypothesis is strongly rejected.

Tukey's multiple comparison test shows SP group differences on EI. The mean differences in group high and low, group average and low on EI and its four dimensions. It mean school provisions (*e.g.*, discipline, Book bank, Facilities for poor students, cultural activities, sports and other facilities) affects EI of adolescents.

Hypothesis No. 24 was state, 'There exists no significant effect of various levels of school provisions (SP) on adjustment.'

This hypothesis is strongly rejected in the present study. It is observed that three groups of SP are significantly different on adjustment.

In Tukey's multiple comparison test SP group differences observed on adjustment. It means that if school provisions are good, the adjustment is excellent. On the contrasy SP is low adolescents adjustment is poor.

Hypothesis No. 25 was formulated that, 'There exists no significant effect of various levels of academic provisions (AP) on emotional intelligence (EI).

Table 4.54 depicts that three levels of AP perceived by the adolescents significantly affects on EI. So null hypothesis no. 25 is strongly rejected.

In Tukey's multiple comparison test (Table 4.56) AP group difference found on EI. It means that high academic provision supports the development of EI of adolescents.

Hypothesis No. 26 stated that, 'There exists no significant effect of various levels of academic provision (AP) on adjustment.'

This hypothesis partially accepted. Table 4.57 indicates that three levels of AP perceived by the adolescents significantly differ on home, health and overall adjustment.

In Tukey's multiple comparison test also shows mean difference in high and average, high and low groups on home, health and overall adjustment. It is interpreted that high AP supports EI of adolescents.

Hypothesis No. 27 formulated that, 'There exists no significant effect of various levels of academic climate (AC) on emotional intelligence (EI).

This hypothesis is strongly rejected. Table 4.60 shows that three levels of AC perceived by adolescents are significantly differ on EI.

Tukey's multiple comparison test (Table 4.62) shows mean difference in all pairs of AC significantly on EI. It means that high academic climate create high emotional intelligence of adolescents. Goleman (1998) reported that family and school are the places which can develop emotional and social competences, that is emotional intelligence.

Hypothesis No. 28 stated that, 'There exists no significant effect of various levels of academic climate (AC) on adjustment.'

This null hypothesis is rejected. Table 4.63 shows that three levels of AC perceived by the adolescents significantly affect home, health, emotional and overall adjustment.

Tukey's multiple comparison test (Table 4.65) indicates mean difference in all pairs of AC (home, health, emotional and overall adjustment). It is interpreted that high AC supports to excellent adjustment of adolescents. Freiberg (1998) suggested that positive school climate can yield positive educational and psychological outcomes for students and school personnel.

Hypothesis No. 29 framed that, 'Parental acceptance attitude and academic climate will be jointly and significantly interact to yield different outcomes of emotional intelligence.'

It is noticed from Table 4.66 different levels of parental acceptance create different output of emotional intelligence. It is also found that an effect of academic climate is statistically significant on emotional intelligence. But interaction of PA x AC found no significant.

Table 4.67 Scheffe's multiple comparison test showed PA group differences on EI. There is significant difference between group high and average, high and low, average and low on EI. Fig. 4.1 also depicted that high PA attitude create high EI of adolescents. On the contrary low PA attitude shows low EI of adolescents. Previous research supported this finding. Mithas (1997) reported that emotional competences were found to be greater in those early adolescents whose perceived mothering was associated with acceptance than rejection.

It was hypothesized No. 30 that, 'Parental concentration (PC) attitude and academic climate will jointly and significantly interact to yield different outcomes of emotional intelligence (EI).'

Table 4.68 depicted that different levels of PC creates different outputs of EI. It is found that PC attitude affects EI. It is also seen that AC affects EI. But interaction of PC x AC is not significant on EI.

In Scheffe's multiple comparison test mean difference of all PC groups found significant. Fig. 4.2 PC levels and EI depicted. It is interpreted that low PC support to develop EI. But when parents concentrating on their children, it becomes an obstacle in their development of EI.

Hypothesis No. 31 stated that, 'Parental avoidance (PV) attitude and academic climate will jointly and significantly interact to yield different outcomes of emotional intelligence (EI).

It is noticed that different levels of PV creates different outputs of EI. It means that PV attitude affects EI. AC also affects EI. But PV and AC jointly and significantly could not yield different outcomes on EI.

Table 4.69 Scheffe's multiple comparison test mean differences of PV groups found significant on EI. Fig. 4.3 PV levels and EI showed that high PV decreased EI and low PV increases EI. It is natural because child develops unpleasant attitude when his parents neglect him.

Hypothesis No. 32 framed that, 'Parental acceptance (PA) attitude and academic climate (AC) will jointly and significantly interact to yield different outcomes of adjustment.'

Table 4.72 depicted that PA attitude does not affect adjustment. But AC affects adjustment. However, interaction effects of PA and AC found non-significant on adjustment.

Table 4.73 in Scheffe's multiple comparison test all PA group differences found non-significant. Fig. 4.4 indicates that high PA create excellent adjustment and low PA create poor adjustment of adolescents.

Table 4.74 denotes that all AC groups found significant mean difference on adjustment. Fig. 4.5 indicates levels of AC and adjustment. High AC supports to good adjustment and on the contray low AC creates poor adjustment in adolescents.

Hypothesis No. 33 'Parental concentration (PC) and academic climate (AC) will be jointly and significantly interacting to yield different outcomes of adjustments.

Table 4.75 denotes that PC attitude affects on adjustment. AC also affects on adjustment. But interaction effect of PC and AC is non-significant.

Table 4.76 Scheffe's test denotes that all PC groups' differences found significant on adjustment. Fig. 4.6 depicted that high PC creates low adjustment and low PC supports excellent adjustment. Concentration or over protection is a disease and obstructs the independent growth of the child.

Hypothesis No. 34 framed that, 'Parental avoidance attitude (PA) and academic climate (AC) will jointly and significantly interact to yield different outcomes of adjustment.

Table 4.77 denotes that PV affects adjustment. AC also affects on adjustment. But interaction effect of PV and AC jointly not significantly affects adjustment.

Table 4.78 in Scheffe's test all PV group mean differences found significant on adjustment. Fig. 4.7 shows that high PV creates poor adjustment and low PV shows good adjustment of adolescents. Previous studies supported this findings. Parental rejection makes children fearful, insecure, jealous, aggressive, hostile and lonely with distorted and devaluated self-image (Coleman, 1970), having emotional instability, poor educational adjustment and more aggressive tendencies (Verma and Bansal, 1989).

In this way, discussion of the study clearly proves that family relationship and academic climate affects emotional intelligence and adjustment of adolescents.

6

SUMMARY, CONCLUSIONS AND RECOMMENDATIONS

Introduction

Present study is conducted to examine the effects of family relationship and academic climate on emotional intelligence and adjustment of adolescents. A review of literature on selected variables has been carried out and it has been observed that family relationship and academic climate affects on emotional intelligence and adjustment of adolescents. Present chapter contains brief description of variables carried out in the study, aim of the study, objectives, hypothesis, sample, tools, procedure, statistical techniques, conclusions, recommendations and limitations of the study.

Summary of Variables under the Study

Family being the first and major agency of socialization plays a pivotal role in shaping child's life. It has been shown most of the children who are successful and well-adjusted come from families where healthy relationships exit between children and their parents. Family is the first environment place where child feels, observes and learns the emotional relationships (Warhol, 1998). Children try to understand the emotions through the attachment and modeling with parents (Denham *et al*. 2000). The family provides the first context for recognition and communication of affective messages to develop social intelligence and social competence.

Parental acceptance implies an attitude of love for the child. The accepting parent put the child in a position of importance in the home and develops a relationship of emotional warmth. Parental acceptance encourages the child and makes itself apparent in receptive or positive attitude towards the child's idea and judgments, worthiness and capability, love and affection and admiration along with adequate attention towards him.

An avoidance attitude of parents manifests itself in interpersonal relationships in direct ways, when the child has to face excessive criticism, jealousy comparison, harsh and inconsistent punishment by both or either of the parents in his upbringing. An avoidance attitude of parents may also exhibit itself in physical neglect, denial of love and affection, lack of interest in his activities and failure to spend time with him. This attitude of parents implies conditional love, recognizing that child has no right as a person, no right to express his feelings, no right to uniqueness and no right to become autonomous individual.

Protection in the child makes him better and more confident. Reality is that over protection is a disease and obstructs the independent growth of the child. But sense of protection gives the child strength and psychological support. So the sense of protection and over protection both are different. Parent shows over anxiousness towards the child's health and protection him from strong participation in completing activities. Thus overprotection signifies giving more care to their child than what is necessary and can only be deemed as the hyper state of protection.

School is a place where students get together share instructions and social infrastructures, which is fundamental to shaping their interests, attitudes and habits. Many activities in the classroom have an influence on the student's personality. School climate is an important input for building the healthy learning environment. A stimulating educational environment responsive to the needs of the individual can result in positive motivational consequences. On the contrary negative motivational consequences will result if the environment is not facilitative (Chen, 2005; Brock, Nishidk, Choing, Grimm, Rimm – Kaufman, 2008).

According to Goleman, emotional intelligence refers to the ability to recognize and regulate emotions in ourselves and others. Salovy and Mayer (1997) defined, emotional intelligence "the ability to perceive emotion, integrate emotions and to facilitate thought, understand emotions and to regulate emotions to promote personal growth. In brief we can say that emotional intelligence refers to emotional reasoning used to understand and manage the expressions of emotions of self and others.

The concept of adjustment is as old as human race on earth. The process of adjustment starts from the birth of child and is continuous till his/her death. Psychologists use term 'adjustment' 'varying' conditions of social or interpersonal relationship in the society. Adjustment means reaction to the demands and pressures of social environment imposed upon the individual. The demand may be external or internal to whom the individual to react. Adjustment means reaction to the demands and pressures of social environment imposed upon the individual. The demand may be external or internal to whom the individual to react (Agarwal 1996).

Aim of the Study

Family and school is undivided part of every student's life. Most of their time, they spend in school and family. School and teacher teach him, how to live in the competitive life with well adjustment by knowing own motives, and emotions. Hence the main aim of the study was to find out the effect of family relationship, and academic climate on emotional intelligence and adjustment of adolescents.

Objectives of the Study

Some major objectives were kept for present research works as under.

1. To find out the difference between male and female adolescents on their mothers and fathers acceptance, concentration and avoidance attitude.

2. To search the difference between male and female adolescents perception on various components of academic climate.
3. To investigate the difference between male and female adolescents on various dimensions of emotional intelligence.
4. To search the difference between male and female adolescents on various areas of adjustment.
5. To find out the difference between urban and rural adolescents perception on their mothers and fathers acceptance, concentration and avoidance attitude.
6. To search the difference between urban and rural adolescents perception on their various dimensions of academic climate.
7. To find out the difference between urban and rural adolescents on various dimensions of emotional intelligence.
8. To examine the difference between urban and rural adolescents on various areas of adjustment.
9. To search the effects of various levels of parental acceptance, concentration and avoidance attitude on emotional intelligence of adolescents.
10. To examine the effect of various dimensions of academic climate on emotional intelligence of adolescents.
11. To find out the effect of various levels of parental acceptance, concentration and avoidance attitude on adjustment of adolescents.
12. To search the effect of various dimensions of academic climate on adjustment of adolescents.
13. To study the main and interaction effect of family relationship (parents acceptance attitude towards their child) and academic climate on emotional intelligence.
14. To investigate the main and interaction effect of family relationship (concentration) and academic climate on emotional intelligence of adolescents.

15. To see the main and interaction effect of family relationship (avoidance attitudes) and academic climate on emotional intelligence of adolescents.
16. To explore the main and interaction influence of family relationship (acceptance attitudes) and academic climate on adjustment of adolescents.
17. To search the main and interaction impact of family relationship (concentration attitudes) and academic climate on adjustment of adolescents.
18. To investigate the main and interaction effect of family relationship (avoidance attitude) and academic climate on adjustment of adolescents.

Hypotheses of the Study

Following hypotheses were tested in the study.

1. Male and Female adolescents would not differ on their mothers and fathers acceptance attitude.
2. There will be no significant difference between male and female adolescents on their mothers and fathers concentration attitude.
3. There would be no significant difference between male and female adolescents on their mothers and fathers avoidance attitude.
4. There would be no significant difference between male and female adolescents perception on various components of academic climate.
5. There will be no significant difference between male and female adolescents on various dimensions of emotional intelligence.
6. There will be no significant difference between male and female adolescents on various areas of adjustment.
7. There will be no significant difference between urban and rural adolescents on their mothers and fathers acceptance attitude.
8. There will be no significant difference between urban and rural adolescents on their mothers and fathers concentration attitude.

9. There will be no significant difference between urban and rural adolescents on their mothers and fathers avoidance attitude.
10. There would be no significant difference between urban and rural adolescents perception on their various dimensions of academic climate.
11. There will be no significant difference between urban and rural adolescents on various dimensions of emotional intelligence.
12. There will be no significant difference between urban and rural adolescents on various areas of adjustment.
13. The various levels of parental acceptance will yield different outcomes of emotional intelligence of adolescents.
14. There is no significant effect on adjustment of various levels of parental acceptance of adolescents.
15. There exists no significant effect of levels of parental concentration on emotional intelligence of adolescents.
16. There exists no significant effect of various levels of parental concentration on adjustment of adolescents.
17. There exists no significant effect of various levels of parental avoidance attitude on emotional intelligence and its four dimensions.
18. There exists no significant effect of various levels of parental avoidance on adjustment and its four areas.
19. There exists no significant effect of various levels of physical material (a dimension of academic climate) on emotional intelligence.
20. There exists no significant effect of various levels of physical material (a dimension of academic climate) on adjustment.
21. There exists no significant effect of various levels of Inter personal Trust (a dimension of academic climate) on emotional intelligence.
22. There exists no significant effect of various levels of Inter personal Trust (a dimension of academic climate) on adjustment.

23. There exists no significant effect of various levels of School Provisions (a dimension of academic climate) on emotional intelligence.
24. There exists no significant effect of various levels of school provisions (a dimension of academic climate) on adjustment.
25. There exists no significant effect of various levels of academic provisions (a dimensions of academic climate) on emotional intelligence.
26. There exists no significant effect of various levels of academic provisions (a dimensions of academic climate) on adjustment.
27. There exists no significant effect of various levels of academic climate on emotional intelligence.
28. There exists no significant effect of various levels of academic climate on adjustment.
29. Parental acceptance attitude and academic climate will jointly and significantly interact to yield different outcomes of emotional intelligence.
30. Parental concentration attitude and academic climate will jointly and significantly interact to yield different outcomes of emotional intelligence.
31. Parental avoidance attitude and academic climate will jointly and significantly interact to yield different outcomes of emotional intelligence.
32. Parental acceptance attitude and academic climate will jointly and significantly interact to yield different outcomes of adjustment.
33. Parental concentration attitude and academic climate will jointly and significantly interact to yield different outcomes of adjustment.
34. Parental avoidance attitude and academic climate will jointly and significantly interact to yield different outcomes of adjustment.

Sample

Present research has been conducted in three districts of Western Maharashtra *viz*; Sangli, Satara and Kolhapur. 847 students of 11th class has been selected by random sampling method for this research. The ratio of the sample among these three districts was kept as 1:1:1. Students studying in 11th class were selected on the basis of gender and residence. The ratio of these two criteria was 1:1 and the varied in age range from 16 to 17 years. 30 Junior colleges among Sangli, Satara and Kolhapur districts have been visited to collect the sample students.

Tools used for Data Collection

Following standardized psychological scales were used to collect the data.

Family Relationship Inventory (FRI)

Family Relationship Inventory is prepared by Sherry and Sinha (1987) on the basis of Brunken and Crites's 'Family Relationship Inventory' in the Indian situations. An inventory may well discriminate the individuals who feel emotionally accepted, over protected or rejected by their parents. The inventory contains 150 items classified into three patterns of mother and father separately. Scoring table is given on the first page of the inventory. For every true response one mark is to be given and marks obtained by the respondents are summed up area wise. A high score in each area of the inventory indicated a high degree of one's feelings of his being accepted, concentrated or avoided by his mother or father or both parents. Test-retest reliability and validity of inventory is moderately high.

Academic Climate Description Questionnaire (ACDQ)

This questionnaire is developed by Shah and Shah (1988). It consists 84 items. The scale have four dimensions with 16 items for physical material, 14 items for interpersonal trust, 32 items for school provisions and 22 items for academic provisions. The students are required to tick only one response of the three given alternatives for each item. It's scoring procedure is very simple. The responses are scored as follows:

1. 2 for the positive statement [response alternative (A)].
2. 1 for the neutral statement [response alternative (B)].
4. 0 for negative statement [response alternative (C)].
5. Thus, the maximum score is 168 and the minimum is zero. High score indicates high academic climate while low score indicates low academic climate. Test has split half reliability value is 0.85 and test-retest reliability found 0.78. Test has high content validity.

Mangal Emotional Intelligence Inventory (MEII)

This inventory developed by S. K. Mangal and Shubhra Mangal (2004). The inventory has 100 items with 'Yes' or 'No' alternatives. This inventory has four aspects namely: *(i)* Intrapersonal awareness, *(ii)* Interpersonal awareness, *(iii)* Intrapersonal management and *(iv)* Interpersonal Management. It is forced choice inventory. The response 'yes' is indicate the presence of emotional intelligence and 'No' for the lack of emotional intelligence. There are some items of adverse meaning. Reliability measured by split-half, K-R formula and test-retest methods and found quiet high that in neat about 0.90. Validity assessed by factorial and criterion approach and found quiet high.

Bell's Adjustment Inventory

This inventory is developed by Dr. R. K. Ojha (1994). This inventory includes four parts: *(i)* Home, *(ii)* Health, *(iii)* Social and *(iv)* Emotional. Each part has 35 statements which are answered 'Yes' or 'No'. Scoring of inventory is most easy. The 'yes' responses are counted. For each 'yes' response 1 score is to be given. The total number of 'yes' scores thus make total score of the individual in the part. The inventory is totally negative inventory. When an individual answers in 'yes', it indicates his difficulties. Reliability is measured by split-half and test-retest method and average of reliability on all dimensions are above 0.85 which is very high. Validity of this inventory is above 0.75. High score on this inventory denotes unsatisfactory adjustment while low score denotes excellent adjustment.

Procedure of Data Collection

For administering the psychological scales first permission of the heads of the Junior Colleges were sought. After completion of these formalities the selected subjects of that Jr. College were collected in a class room where 20 to 25 subjects could sit comfortably and sufficient distance could be kept between the two subjects. So that one could not see the responses written by other. Once the subjects sat comfortably, through informal talk, rapport formation was done. Once, it was found that the subjects are ready to take the psychological scale; first copies of 'Family Relationship Inventory' were distributed among them. The subjects were given standard instructions laid by inventory.

After completing 'Family Relationship Inventory' short rest of five minutes was given the subjects. After it, they were asked to start to respond second scale 'Academic Climate Description Questionnaire' (ACDQ). After completion of this scale subjects were given five minutes rest.

In the next session the subjects were asked to respond third scale 'Mangle Emotional Intelligence Inventory'. After completion of this scale final scale copies of 'Bell's Adjustment Inventory' were distributed among the subjects. Similar procedure was adopted for collecting data from different groups of subjects.

Statistical Treatment of Data

Data analysis is carried out with the help of 'Statistical Package for the Social Sciences (SPSS)'. After collecting the data, all psychological scales were hand scored by the researcher.

First, the data were treated by mean, S.D. and 't' test. *Secondly* One-way ANOVA was used for examining, whether the groups differ significantly or not. Two-way ANOVA was used to see the main and interaction effects of independent variables. Finally, post-hock comparison was done to see the intergroup mean differences are significant or not.

Conclusions

Present study thirty four hypotheses were tested and on the basis of results following conclusions were drawn.

1. There is no significant difference between male and female adolescents on their parental acceptance attitude.
2. There is no significant difference between male and female adolescents on their parental concentration attitude. But it is found that fathers are more concentrating on their male adolescents.
3. There is no significant difference between male and female adolescents on their parental avoidance attitude. Parents showed more avoidance attitude to males than females.
4. It is found that female adolescents' perception of their academic climate is better than male adolescents.
5. There is no significant difference between male and female adolescents on overall emotional intelligence. But there is a significant difference between male and female adolescents on interpersonal management. Females have more ability to interpersonal management than male adolescents.
6. It is found that there is no significant difference between male and female adolescents on overall adjustment. But female adolescents showed good adjustment in social and home area. Males showed good adjustment in emotional area of adjustment.
7. There is no significant difference between urban and rural adolescents on their parental acceptance attitude.
8. It is found that there is no significant difference between urban and rural adolescents' perception on their parental concentration attitude. But fathers of rural area are more concentrating on their adolescent children than urban fathers.
9. There is significant difference between urban and rural adolescents' perception on their parental avoidance attitude. Rural parents have more avoiding attitude than urban parents.

10. There is no significant difference between urban and rural adolescents' perception on overall academic climate. It is also found that there is significant difference between urban and rural adolescents' on school and academic provisions. Rural adolescents perceived that their schools are not providing school and academic facilities as compare to urban schools.
11. There is no significant difference between urban and rural adolescents on emotional intelligence.
12. There is significant difference between urban and rural adolescents on adjustment. Urban adolescents have better adjustment than rural adolescents.
13. It is found that a parental acceptance level significantly affects emotional intelligence of adolescents. Parental high acceptance attitude increases emotional intelligence than average and low level of PA attitude.
14. It is observed that three groups of parental acceptance attitude (PA) are significantly varied on home and social adjustment. It means that PA affects home and social adjustment of adolescents. High PA creates excellent adjustment and low PA creates poor adjustment in adolescents.
15. It is found that levels of parental concentration attitude are significantly different on emotional intelligence. Level of PC affects EI. High PC creates low EI and low PC supports to development of EI in adolescents.
16. It is seen that levels of PC affects overall adjustment of adolescents. High PC creates poor adjustment, while average and low PC creates excellent adjustment of adolescents.
17. Research revealed that parental avoidance attitude (PV) significantly affects emotional intelligence of adolescents. It is found that high PV negatively influence on development of EI of adolescents.
18. Study revealed that PV significantly affects adjustment of adolescents. High PV significantly creates poor adjustment in adolescents than average and low PV.

19. It is found that levels of physical material (PM) significantly affects EI of adolescents. High PM showed high EI, while low PM showed poor EI of adolescents.
20. It is seen that levels of PM significantly affect home, health and overall adjustment. High PM create high adjustment, while low PM creates poor adjustment in adolescents.
21. It is found that levels of IPT significantly affect EI of adolescents. High IPT creates high EI and low IPT creates low EI of adolescents.
22. Study revealed that levels of IPT significantly affect adjustment of adolescents. High IPT results excellent adjustment, while low IPT create poor adjustment of adolescents.
23. It is seen that levels of SP significantly affect EI. High SP supports to EI, while low SP creates low EI of adolescents.
24. It is observed that levels of SP significantly affect adjustment. High SP creates good adjustment, while low SP creates poor adjustment of adolescents.
25. It is found that various levels of AP significantly affect EI. High AP shows high EI, while low AP shows low EI of adolescents.
26. It is seen that levels of AP significantly affect adjustment. It means that high AP supports good adjustment while low AP creates poor adjustment of adolescents.
27. It is found that levels of AC significantly affect EI. It means that high AC creates high EI, while low AC creates low EI of adolescents.
28. Study revealed that levels of AC significantly affect adjustment of adolescents. It means that high AC supports good adjustment, while low AC results poor adjustment of adolescents.
29. It is seen that no interaction effect of parental acceptance attitude (PA) and academic climate (AC) found significant on EI of adolescents.

30. It is found that no interaction effect of parental concentration attitude (PC) on academic climate (AC) found significant on EI of adolescents.
31. There is no interaction effect of parental avoidance attitude (PV) and academic climate (AC) found significant on EI of adolescents.
32. There is no interaction effect of parental acceptance attitude (PC) and academic climate (AC) found significant on adjustment of adolescents.
33. It is found that no interaction effect of parental concentration attitude (PC) and academic climate (AC) found significant on adjustment of adolescents.
34. An interaction effect of parental avoidance attitude (PV) and academic climate (AC) found non-significant on adjustment of adolescents.

Recommendations

The following recommendations are suggested on the basis of present research.

1. It is recommended that Government should provide good infrastructure to every school and college. It is essential to develop students' cognitive abilities.
2. There is need to framing the curriculum in a way that, emotional intelligence, family relationship and various areas of adjustment should be included. It will be helpful to every student in day to day behaviour.
3. Every school and college teacher should know the importance of emotional intelligence. For this purpose teacher training camps and workshops should be arranged.
4. Government should appoint at least one psychological counselor for every schools and college to solve the psychological problems of the students.
5. Government should assign the responsibility to any psychological organization to search the levels of emotional intelligence of high school and college students in various regions of Maharashtra.

6. Every school and college should form teacher-parent association. Parents' should introduce the importance of parent-child relationship in personality development and behaviour of the children.
7. It is recommended that larger and more representative sample should be used to generalize the results of present study.

Limitations

Before generalizing the findings of the study a few limitations should be taken into consideration.

1. Number of factors affect emotional intelligence and adjustment of adolescents but present study only family relationship and academic climate has been considered.
2. Sample was selected from 11th standard of Arts, Science and Commerce only and not included senior college and P.G., students.
3. Sample was collected from Sangli, Satara and Kolhapur districts only.
4. Sample was small; results may be changed for large sample.

BIBLIOGRAPHY

Abdullah and Maria (2008). Contribution of Emotional Intelligence, Coping and Social Support towards Adjustment and Academic Achievement amongst Fresh Students in the University. PhD. Thesis Unpublished. *University Putra Malaysia.*

Abisamra, N. (2000). The Relationship between Emotional Intelligence and Academic Achievement in Eleventh Grades. *Research in Education,* FED. 661.

Adams, D. Y. K., and Bennion, L. D. (1990). Parent – Adolescent Relationship and Identity Formation. In B. K. Baber and B. C. Rollins (Eds.), *Parent – Adolescent Relationship,* pp. 1-6. Lenham, M.D.: University Press America.

Adsul, Ramesh K. (2013). A Comparative Study of Urban and Rural Students on Emotional Intelligence and Adjustment. *Indian Journal of Positive Psychology,* Vol. 4 (1), 169-171.

Aggrwal, J. C. (1996). Essentials of Educational Psychology. *New Delhi:* Vikas Publishing House Pvt. Ltd.

Alegre, A. (2011). Parenting Styles and Children's Emotional Intelligence: What Do We Know?. *The Family Journal: Counselling and Therapy for Couples and Families,* 19(1), 56-62.

Ara, N. (1986). Parent's Personality, Child Rearing Attitude and their Children's Personality. An Interconnectional Study. *Unpublished Doctoral Dissertation*, Bhagalpur University, Bhagalpur.

Badani, H. D., and Goswami, S. P. (1973). Social Adjustment in Relation to Some Organic and Environmental Variables. *Journal of Education and Psychology,* 31, 74-79.

Baker, J. A. (2006). Contributions of Teacher – Child Relationships to Positive School Adjustment during Elementary School. *Journal of School Psychology,* 44, 211-229.

Bar-on, R. (1997). Emotional Intelligence Quotient Inventory: A Measure of Emotional Intelligence, Toronto, Multilealth Systems, Inc.

Battistich, V., Schps, E., and Willson, N. (2004). Effects of an Elementary School Intervention on Students 'Connectedness' to School and Social Adjustment during Middle School. *The Journal of Primary Prevention,* 24 (3), 243-262.

Begley, N., and Schaefer, E. S. (1960). Maternal Behaviour and Personality Development. *IOWA City Regional Research Council on Child Development and Child Psychiatry.*

Biradar, Shweta (2006). The Analysis of Parenting Style and Emotional Intelligence of the College Students. Thesis *Submitted to the University of Agricultural Sciences, Dharwad.*

Brackett, M., and Mayer, J. D. (2003). Convergent, Discriminate and Incremental Validity of Competing Measures of Emotional Intelligence. *Personality and Social Psychology Bulletin,* 29, 1147-1158.

Brock, L. L., Nishida T. K., Chiong C; Griamm, K. J. , Rimm-Kaufman S. E. (2008). Children's Perceptions of the Classroom Environment and Social Academic Performance: A Longitudinal Analysis of the Contribution of the Responsive Classroom Approach. *School Psychology.* 46 (2), 129-149.

Cabrera, N. J., Tamis – Lemonda, C. S, Bradley, R. H., Hoffrth, S., and Lamb, M.E (2000). *Fatherhood in the Twenty First Century: Child Development.* 71: 127-136.

Chakra, A and Prabha, R. (2004). Influence of Family Environment on Competence Adolescents. *Journal of Community Guidance and Research,* 21, 2,213-222.

Charlson, M. J. (2006). Family Structure, Father Involvement and Adolescent Behavioural Outcomes. *Journal of Marriage and Family,* 68, 137-154.

Chen, J. J. (2005). Relation to Academic Support from Parents, Teachers and Peers to Hong Kong Adolescents' Academic Achievement: The Meditating Role of Academic Engagement. *Genetics Sociology, General Psychology Monograph,* 131(2), 77-127.

Chu (2002). Boys Development. *Reader's Digest*, 94-95.

Colemen, J. C. (1970). Abnormal Psychology and Modern Life. Bombay, D. B. Taraporwala and Sons.

Croninger, R. G., and Lee V. E. (2001). Social Capital and Dropping out of High School: Benefits to At – Risk Students of Teachers' Support and Guidance. *Teacher College Record* 103(4), 548-58.

Crosnoe (2002). Protective Functions of Family Relationships and School Factors on the Deviant Behaviour of Adolescent Boys and Girls: Reducing the Impact of Risky Friendships. *Youth and Society,* 33,4, 515-544.

Dash, M., and Neena Dash (2006). Fundamental of Educational Psychology. New Delhi; Atlantic Publishers.

David, A. A. (2004). The Buffering Effect of Emotional Intelligence on the Adjustment of Secondary School Students in Transition. *Electronic Journal of Research in Educational Psychology*. 6,3,(2), 79-90.

Deepshikha and Suman, Bhanot (2009). Role of Family Environment in Social Adjustment of Adolescent Girls in Rural Areas of Eastern U.P. *Indian Journal of Social Science Researches,* Vol. 6. 2.

Denham, S. A.; Workman, E.; Cole, P. M. (2000). Prediction of Externalizing Behaviour Problems from Early to Middle Childhood: The Role of Parental Socialization and Emotion Expression. *Development and Psychopathology,* 12,23-45.

Donohue, K. M., Perry, K. E., and Weinstein. R. S (2003). Teachers Classroom Practices and Children's Rejection by their Peers. *Applied Developmental Psychology,* 24, 91-118.

Doyle A. B. and Moretti, M. M. (2000). Attachment to Parents and Adjustment in Adolescence. Health Canada, File No. 032ss. H5219-00CYH3.

Erickson, E (1968). Identity Youth and Crises, Norton, New York.

Fatos, Erkman and Aysen, E.(2011). Parental Acceptance – Rejection Theory and Interpersonal Acceptance and Rejection in Social, Emotional and Educational Contexts. *International Society for Interpersonal Acceptance – Rejection.* Boca Raton, Florida, USA.

Fields, Jason and Lynne, Casper (2001). American's Families and Living Arrangements, Current Population. Series p. 20-537.

File: //c:\Documents and settings/National school climate center school... 2/3/2013.School Climate (Academic Climate).

File://D\National school climate centre school climate Research.ltd 2/3/2013 Academic Climate.

Finnegam, J. E. (1998). Measuring Emotional Intelligence: Where we are Today. Montgomery, A.L: Anbum University of Montgomery, School of Education. *ERTC Document Reproduction Service No. E D 42608.*

Freberge, H. J. (1998). Measuring School Climate: Late me Count the Ways. *Educational Leadership,* 56,1,22-26.

Glick, Paul C. (1957). American Families. New York: John Wiley.

Golman, Daniel (1995). Emotional Intelligence: Why it can Matter Mare than IQ. Bantam Books, New York.

Good C. V. (1959). Dictionary of Education. New York: McGraw Hill Book Company.

Guy, Claxton (2005). An Intelligent look at Emotional Intelligence. *Association of Teachers and Lecturers,* University of Bristol.

Haynes, N., M., and Comer, J. P. (1993). The Yele School Development Programme Process, Outcomes and Policy Implications. *Urban Education*, 28,2,166-199.

Hoffman, M. L. (1960). Power Association by the Parent and Its Impact on the Child. *Child Development*, 31, 129-143.

Jay, P., and Singh, S. (1991). A Study on Neurotic Tendencies as a Result of Perceived Parental Rejection. *Indian Psychological Review*, 37,7,11-17.

Joshi, Renuka and Sharma, Manju (2013). Emotional Intelligence among Boys and Girls. Indian *Journal of Health and Well-being*. Vol. 4(2), 374-375.

Jossey-Bass. (2009). Adolescent Health: Understanding and Preventing Risk Behaviour.

Katyal, S., and Awasthi, E. (2005). Gender Differences in Emotional Intelligence among Adolescents of Chandhigarh, Kamal-Raj, J. Hum. Ecol., 17 (2), 153-155.

Klem, A. M., and Connell, J. P. (2004). Relationships Matter: Linking Teacher Support to Student Engagement and Achievement. *Journal of School Health*. 74(7), 262-273.

Kulshrestha, S. P. (1979). Educational Psychology. Meerut, India: Loyal Book Depot.

Kuperminc, G. P. and Blatt, S. J. (1997). Perceived School Climate and Difficulties in the Social Adjustment of Middle School Students. *Applied Developmental Science*, 1,2,76-88.

Lamb, M. E. (2004). The Role of the Father in Child Development. New York: Wiley.

Lopez, F. G. (1991). Pattern of Family Conflict and their Relation to College Student Adjustment. *Journal of Counselling and Development*, 69,3,257-260.

Maehr (1990). The 'Psychological Environment' of the School: A Focus of School Leaderships. Project Report Urbana. Illinois: *National Center for School Leadership*. ED 327954.

Malhotra Palak and Sihotra Kranti (2013). A Comparative Study of Emotional Maturity and Adjustment Level of College Students. *Indian Journal of Health and Well-being*. Vol. 4 (2), 368-370.

Mangal S. K. (2010). Essentials of Educational Psychology. PHI Learning Pvt. Ltd. New Delhi.

Mangal, S. K., and Mangal Shubhra (2004). Mangal Emotional Intelligence Inventory. *National Psychological Corporation,* Agra, India.

Mangal, S.K. (1999). Advanced Educational Psychology. New Delhi; Prentice Hall of India Private Limited.

Manning, M. L., and Saddlemire, R. (1996). Developing a Sense of Community in Secondary Schools. National Association of Secondary School Principals. *NASSP Bulletin,* 80,584, 41-48.

Martinez-Pons, Manuel (1999). Parental Inducement of Emotional Intelligence. *Imagination, Cognition and Personality,* 18,1, 3-23.

Mayer, J. D., Dipaoio, M. and Salovey, P. (1990). Perceiving Affective Content in Ambiguous Visual Stimulating Emotional Intelligence. *Journal of Personality Assessment* 54,772-781.

Mayer, J. D., and Salovey, P. (1997). What is Emotional Intelligence? In P. Salovey and D. J. Sluyter (Eds.), Emotional Development and Emotional Intelligence: *Educational Implications.* 3-31, New York: Basic Books.

Mayer, Dioaolo and Salovey (1990). Perceiving Affective Content in Ambiguous Visual Stimulating Emotional Intelligence. *Journal of Personality Assessment* 54,772-781.

McEvoy, A., and Welker, R. (2000). Antisocial Behaviour, Academic Failure, and School Climate: A Critical Review. *Journal of Emotional and Behavioural Disorders,* 8,3,130-140.

Mithas, U. J. (1997). Parenting Models and Sex as Correlates of Emotional Competence among Early Adolescent Labourer and Non-Labourer. *Doctoral Dissertation, (Unpublished.) Agra.*

Morris, A. S.; Silk, J. S. Steinberg, L.; Mayers, S. S. and Robinson, L. R. (2007). The Role of the Family Context in the Development of Emotion Regulation. *Social Development,* 16, 2, 361-368.

Nihara, K. T., and Oshio, Y. (1987). Homes of TMR Children: Comparison between American and Japanese Families. *American Journal of Mental Deficiency,* 91,486-195.

Ojha, R., K. (1994). Bell's Adjustment Inventory. *National Psychological Corporation*, Agra, India.

Perry, A. (1908). The Management of a City School, New York, McMillan.

Raikes, H. A., and R. A. Thompson (2006). Family Emotional Climate, Attachment Security and Young Children's Emotion Knowledge in a High Risk Sample. *British Journal of Developmental Psychology,* 24, 1, 89-104.

Raju M. V. K. and T. Khaja Rahamtulla (2007). Adjustment Problems among School Students. *Journal of Indian Academy of Applied Psychology.* 33, (1), 73-79.

Rimm-Kaufman, S. E., and Chiu,Y. I. (2007). Promoting Social and Academic Competence in the Classroom. An Intervention Study Examining the Contribution of the Responsive Classroom Approach. *Psychology in the Schools,* 44(4), 397-413.

Rimm-Kaufman, S. E., Early ,D., Cox, M., Saluja G., Pianta, R, Bradely, R. *et al*. (2002). Early Behaviour Attributes and Teachers 'Sensitivity as Predictors' Competent Behaviour in the Kindergarten Classroom. *Journal of Applied Developmental Psychology,* 23 451-470.

Rudasill, K. M, Rimm-Kaufman, S. E, Justice, L. M and Pence, K. (2006). Temperament and Language Skills as Predictors of Teachers – Child Relationship Quality in Preschool. *Early Education and Development,* 17(2), 271-291.

Safavi, H. Mousavi L.S., Lotfi, R. (2008). Correlation between Emotional Intelligence and Socio-emotional Adjustment in Pre-university Girl Students in Tehran. *Pajoohandeh Journal,* 1, 5,255-261.

Saha, M. L., and Shah, Amita (1988). Academic Climate Description Questionnaire (ACDQ). *Ankur Psychological Agency*, Lucknow, India.

Salovey, P., and Mayer, J. D. (1990). Emotional Intellience. Imagination, Cognition and Personality, 9, 185-211.

Shakuntala Punia and Santosh Sagwan (2011). Emotional Intelligence and Social Adaptation of School Children Kamla-Raj, *J Psychology,* 2[2]: 83-87.

Sharma Aditi (2013). Influence of Family Climate, Relations with Peers and Adjustment on Adolescents' Well-being. *Indian Journal of Health and Well-being.* Vol. 4 (1), 68-71.

Sharma Anita, Sharma Jyoti and Pal Krishnal (2013). Family Environment As a Predictor of Adjustment in Adolescents. *Indian Journal of Health and Well-being.* Vol. 4(3), 437-443.

Sharpiro, L. E. (2000). How to Rise a Child with High Emotional Intelligence. Istanbul: Verlik Publication.

Shashidhar, S. Rao, C. Hegade , R. (2009). Factors Affecting Scholastic Performances of Adolescents. *Indian Journal of Pediatrics.* 76 (5), 495-499.

Sherry, G., P. and Sinha, J. C. (1987). Family Relationship Inventory. *National Psychological Corporation*, Agra, India.

Shukla Richa and Nagar Dinesh (2013). Impact of Gender and Managerial Levels on Emotional Intelligence and Job Performance of Indian Revenue Service officers. *Indian Journal of Health and Well-being,* Vol. 4 (1), 83-86.

Sim, T. (2003). The Father – Adolescent Relationship in the Context of the Mother – Adolescent Relationship: Exploring Moderating Linkages in a Late Adolescent Sample in Singapore. *Journal of Adolescent Resaerch,* 18, 4, 383-404.

Singh (2002). Emotional Intelligence at Work : A Professional Guide. New Delhi: Sage Publications.

Singh, Dheeraj and Sahu, Kiran (2013). Psychological Well-being and Emotional Intelligence among Adolescents Boys and Girls. *Indian Journal of Health and Well-being.* Vol. 4(1), 38-40.

Subbu, S., and Jangaiah, C. (2005). Adjustment and Teachers Stress. *Edutracks,* 5,1,32-35.

Surekha (2008). Relationship between Students Adjustment and Academic Achievement. *Edutracs* 7,7,26-31.

Susan, B. Gall (1998). The Gale Encyclopedia of Childhood and Adolescence. Detroit New York Toronto, London.

Thompson, R. A. (1998). Early Socio-Personality Development. In W. Damon (Series Ed.) and N. Eisenberg (Vol. Ed.), Handbook of Child Psychology. *Social and Personality Development*. Vol. 3, pp. 25-104. New York: Wiley.

Umadevi and Rayal (2005). Relationship between the Dimensions of Emotional Intelligence of Adolescent and Selected Personal Social Variables. *Indian Psychological Review,* 64, 1,11-20.

Vaidya, Alpana (2013). Quality of Life and Emotional Intelligence among Arts and Commerce Students. *Indian Journal of Positive Psychology*. Vol. 4(2), 337-339.

Vamadevappa, H. V. (2005). Adjustment of Over Achievers and under Achievers, 35,1,46-49.

Warhol, J. G. (1998). Facilitating and Encouraging Healthy Emotional Development. *Pediatries,* 102, 5, 1330-1331.

Wing and Love (2001). Elective Affinities and Uninvited Agonies: Mapping Emotions with Significant others onto Health, Emotion. *Social Relationships and Health Series in Affective Science*. New York: Oxford University Press.

Woolf, M. D. (1963). A Study of Some Relationship between Home Adjustment and the Behaviour of Junior College Students. *Journal of Social Psychology,* 17, 275-26.

INDEX

****